MARKER
RENDERING

MARKER RENDERING

FOR FASHION, ACCESSORIES, AND HOME FASHIONS

BINA ABLING

Parsons School of Design
and
Fashion Institute of Technology

Fairchild Publications, Inc.
New York

Executive Editor: Olga T. Kontzias
Assistant Acquisitions Editor: Jaclyn Bergeron
Senior Development Editor: Amy Zarkos
Art Director: Adam B. Bohannon
Production Manager: Ginger Hillman
Associate Production Editor: Beth Cohen
Copy Editor: Roberta Mantus
Cover Design: Susan C. Day
Design and Layout: Susan C. Day
Cover Art: Bina Abling
Photography: Fred Gross

Copyright © 2006
Fairchild Publications, Inc.

Library of Congress Catalog Card Number: 2005926492

ISBN: 1-56367-360-6

GST R 133004424

Printed in China

TP11

Contents

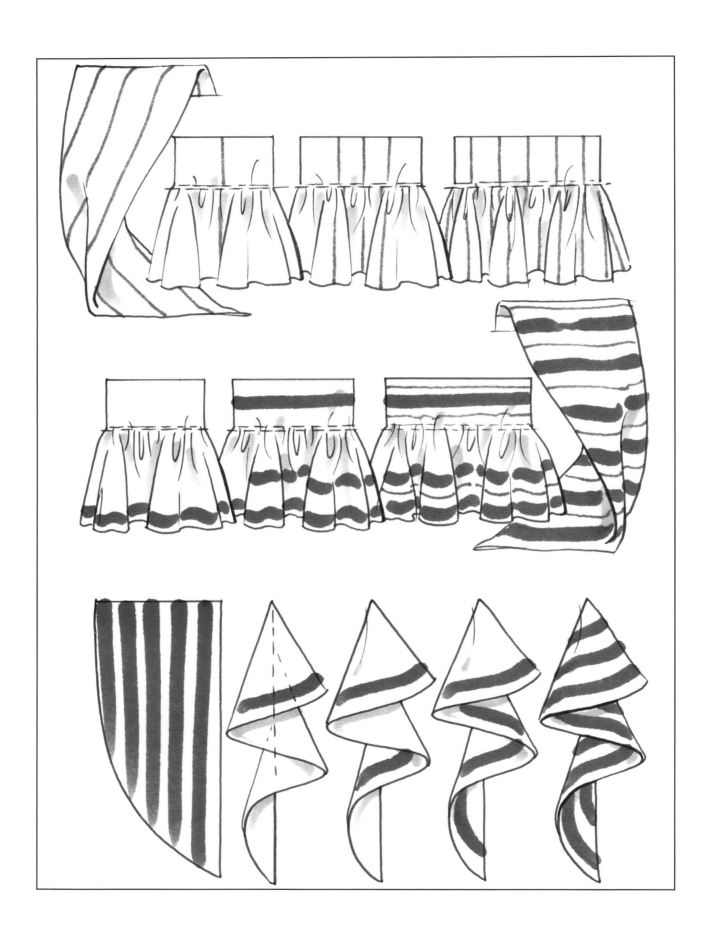

Preface

As the design industry evolves, creative thinking has to be elastic, so as to blend the diverse talents of fashion, accessories, and interior design into one discipline. The current trend of major designers is to include these three disciplines in their licensing agreements, turning apparel, accessories, and home furnishings (surface design) into combined products. New lifestyle magazines are devoted to this trend, their pages filled with this fusion of taste, style, and merchandise.

The goal of this book is to help you to follow this trend by teaching you how to translate your creative thinking into powerful images on paper and to give you the skills you'll need to render your creations like a designer on the job working with deadlines.

The first step in maximizing your design potential is to render your concepts with articulation in line and color. Your illustrations need to be visually dynamic and clear in content to communicate your design direction. This book will give you the basic skills you'll need to develop your talent in marker rendering.

The chapters introduce line, color, and mixed media for markers in a progression that creates a network of skills that will be the tools of your imagination. Designers are always in a rush to express their inspiration. Inspiration needs immediate access to illustration. Markers can give you that spontaneity in a rush of color and accuracy, with just a little practice.

Color accuracy is the latest innovation in markers. The new generation of markers has the full range of the color wheel—tints and shades in a wide variety. Marker color matching has progressed with the addition of nib (point) selection, refills, and the options of mixing your own colors into a blank marker. With marker technology growing, so is the use of markers in the design industry. Portfolios in many design majors for entrance to or graduation from colleges include marker illustrations.

Markers are an excellent choice for color rendering. Adaptable, their rendering can appear dimensional or flat. Their use is compatible with a host of other media. In conjunction with colored pencils and pens, marker illustrations can look polished or rough. Convenient and affordable markers are not as vulnerable to damage as other media. Markers are a basic tool that avoids the cost, care, and cleaning of pastels, gouache, acrylics, or oil paints. Markers do not need extra accessories, setup time or extended drying time between coloring. Plain and simple markers fit into all styles of drawing at any level of expertise.

This book re-creates the classroom experience, asking you to practice with each demonstration, and giving you assignments to challenge your talent in a progression of skills. Using text and illustrations that correspond to a college lecture, the instructions begin slowly and accelerate into advanced skills so that progression is based on proficiency. The colors within each chapter have been kept to a minimum, not just to keep your costs manageable, but for control. You need to learn that marker rendering skills adapt to any color. Keeping it simple gives you the chance to practice without being overwhelmed by color. The diversity in examples should inspire you to look for new design objects to practice rendering.

The methodology in this book is to proceed from the simple to the more complex. You are introduced first to marker rendering basics in Chapters 1–3. You then undertake more complex tasks in Chapters 4 and 5. Chapters 6 and 7 combine more intricate challenges with wider design applications. The appendix is a photo file of fabrics for research and related marker rendering technique notations. Not every fabric covered in the book appears in the appendix. Fabrics that best show detail when photographed are included. Certain types of fabrics appear more than once in the appendix. This is done intentionally to show variety in prints, pattern repeats, or detail.

I used premium 18-pound white marker paper with a smooth surface for my illustrations. Note that I specified marker colors on some pages. Names for the same marker color may vary from company to company. Sometimes a company discontinues a color name and provides a new name for that color. Therefore, I include color names only when they are generic color names used by all marker companies.

I did not list colors used on every page because many colors, especially flesh tones, look slightly different on the printed page than they do on the original artwork. It is often easier to match a given color based on your judgment or available supplies.

Acknowledgments

First I owe a standing ovation to Fairchild Books' executive editor, Olga Kontzias. She performs magic by challenging me to creatively reach beyond my initial concepts. She inspires me with her confidence in my projects to work harder and to achieve better results than I dreamed to be possible. I also applaud the efforts of production editor Beth Cohen for helping me to fine-tune my text. Beth's professionalism is surpassed only by her being calm, which is greatly appreciated, especially when I know I am not. I would like to thank the whole creative team at Fairchild for their input on this book.

Many thanks to the talented people at the marker companies Chartpak Inc., Copic USA, and Prismacolor for the generosity and interest they showed in this project. I asked for their help on this book and they agreed, believing in its educational value, sight unseen. Chartpak Inc. was the first to help, sending some of the most exquisite pastel-colored markers that I have ever used. Thanks to Copic USA for supplying a variety in colors and choices of marker nibs. Their options in marker tips made my job easier. Thanks to Prismacolor for sending the color-coordinated sets of markers and colored pencils, extremely valuable rendering tools for any project. It is obvious in this book that I was enamored with their periwinkle blue, apple green, and crimson red markers and pencils.

I dedicate my chapter-opening photographs to these marker companies for their overall contributions to design education and for their commitment to our artistic expressions in their medium.

I thank Frank Gross for his talents and patience that are evident in his meticulous photography in this book. I love his work as much I love him.

More thanks to Felicia DaCosta for her help with the Fabric Reference and her feedback on my content.

I thank Joshua, Marian, and Brandy at the FIT library for their support and interest in my books. I also sincerely appreciate the efforts of Joe and David, who helped me get the extra supplies I needed for this project from their stores.

Reviewers selected by the publisher were also very helpful. They include Beverly Harkins, Bradley Academy for the Visual Arts; Ann Black, University of Cincinnati; Mary Farahnakian, Brigham Young University; Felicia DaCosta, Parsons School of Design; and Janice McCoart, Marymount University.

Bina Abling

MARKER
RENDERING

CHAPTER 1

INTRODUCTION TO MARKER RENDERING

Checklist for Markers, Pencils, and Pens

Markers   Explore the range (in one color) of marker types. Focus on their efficiency and handling. Efficiency is job-specific. Handling relates to your preference and comfort level. For example, select an extra-wide tip for large areas of color, an ultrafine tip for tiny details, or a contoured nib for both tasks.

Pencils   As you judge markers, you need to determine which brand or type of pencil (usually based on its lead) you like best. There are pencils with thick and thin leads. Thicker lead is softer; thinner leads may be harder. There are also watercolor pencils (for multitasking). Again, you need to explore these types in one color so that you can concentrate on their differences.

Pens   Pens vary in their "mechanics." Essentially, you need to check their ink delivery—too wet, too dry, or tendency to blot. You should also judge a pen on whether you like it—its size, weight, and appearance.

Techniques   As you work with a variety of marker brands, types, or tips, note their qualities and list the pros and cons of each. You can use these four basic rendering methods to test your markers:

- Linear strokes to fill in a space and cover it completely.
- Directed color strokes to create loose or partial rendering that does not fill a space completely.
- Short dabs of color can be used to show texture.
- Scrubbing is a form of filling in. Rub the color over itself so it dries flatter than the directed linear strokes.

Problems   Here are four of the major problems we all run into. They are universal. With practice you will learn to avoid them or use them to your advantage. For example, dry markers work well on great crushed velvets or in letting a color bleed past the outline for a "loose" (expressive) rendering style.

- **Dry color:** Marker is almost empty. Cap was not closed tightly overnight. Marker was left too close to a source of heat.
- **Color streaking or blotching:** Paper could be on wrong side (paper often has a "top" side and a "bottom" side). Fingerprint oils are on the paper surface. The color was worked too slowly. Two different brands of marker were used together (different chemical mixes in their inks).
- **Outline smearing:** The outline edge pen, pencil, or marker is water soluble so it runs. Always test first or buy only nonbleed pens. Or use the outline pen line last, after marker coloring. Or leave more drying time between layers.
- **Color bleeding:** The marker is too full or too wet (as some new, fresh markers can be). Try dabbing the marker with a cotton swab or tissue before use.

Test Page

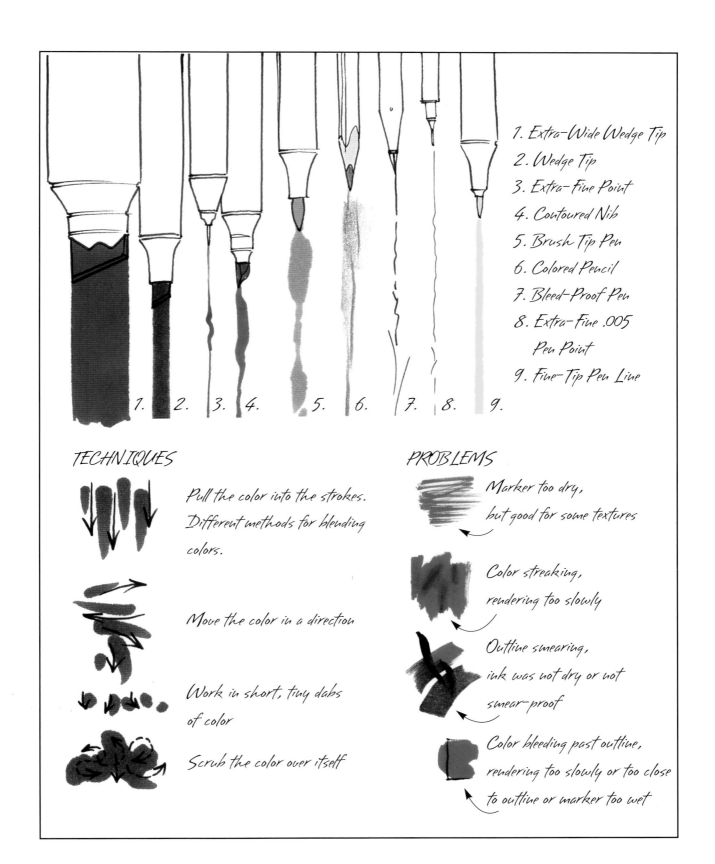

1. Extra-Wide Wedge Tip
2. Wedge Tip
3. Extra-Fine Point
4. Contoured Nib
5. Brush Tip Pen
6. Colored Pencil
7. Bleed-Proof Pen
8. Extra-Fine .005 Pen Point
9. Fine-Tip Pen Line

1. 2. 3. 4. 5. 6. 7. 8. 9.

TECHNIQUES

Pull the color into the strokes. Different methods for blending colors.

Move the color in a direction

Work in short, tiny dabs of color

Scrub the color over itself

PROBLEMS

Marker too dry, but good for some textures

Color streaking, rendering too slowly

Outline smearing, ink was not dry or not smear-proof

Color bleeding past outline, rendering too slowly or too close to outline or marker too wet

Line Variety and Line Quality

The word *line* has at least six inches of definition in the dictionary. Ask an artist to define "line" and you'll get another set of complex definitions starting with line quality. The sheer number of tools dedicated to line drawing is overwhelming. Before you experiment with all kinds of markers, pens, and pencils, just grab one type and get started. It's not about media selection; it's about your developing skills that translate to any media. The skill you need is mastering line quality, either as the exterior or interior segment of your illustration.

Line diversity starts with pressure and release. Pressure on the pen line gives your line its force and intensity. Releasing as you draw gives your line spontaneity and momentum. Together they add visual energy to your rendering, so it won't look static, traced, or dull.

The pen used on the opposite page and throughout this book uses ink that does not bleed. Not all pens have that positive feature. Test any pen after you buy it, to be sure it is bleed-proof, by drawing over marker. Once you know the pen is safe to use for marker rendering, you know there won't be any surprises later on.

There are seven types of line quality on the opposite page. Practice doing these with just one pen, pencil, or marker at a time to examine what that specific pen can and can't do to your satisfaction. This will get you familiar with drawing tools and sketching methods.

Line variety can be greatly influenced by a verbal connection. Think of words that apply to design, and your mind is filled with images. Words can spark your imagination, inspire your drawing, and direct your "line." Try to react creatively to this list. Add more of your own words, and see pages 8 and 9 for some applications of expressive line quality.

- **Frilly:** fringe, feathers, tassels
- **Intricate:** wicker, lace, embroidery
- **Linear:** brickwork, lattice, stripes
- **Nubby:** carpet, knits, terrycloth
- **Raised:** quilting, tapestry, beading
- **Smooth:** porcelain, glass, vinyl
- **Sparkle:** metallics, sequins, jewelry
- **Striated:** marble, granite, wood grain
- **Textured:** faux furs, wooly tweeds

LINE VARIETY

PEN LINE

ROUNDED • ORGANIC • FLOWING

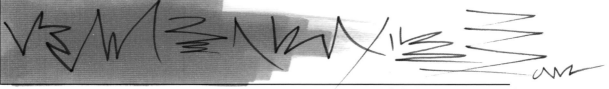

ANGULAR • JAGGED • BROKEN

FINE • LIGHT • DELICATE • FEATHERY

HEAVY • DARK • DENSE • BOLD

MIXED • VARIED • EXPRESSIVE

CHUNKY • RAGGED • IRREGULAR

MIXED • DECORATIVE • EXPRESSIVE

Line Definition

Line definition pushes line quality into function and emphasizes detail, pattern, or texture for a specific image. As your skills grow, your line becomes a unique blend of style and information. Since design illustration, as a business or portfolio presentation, is a tool to express concept and direction, it's up to you to pursue clarity and control. Innovation and creativity in drawing starts with line. Here are some types of lines to practice. They deliver a mix of images that are open to a wide range of interpretation.

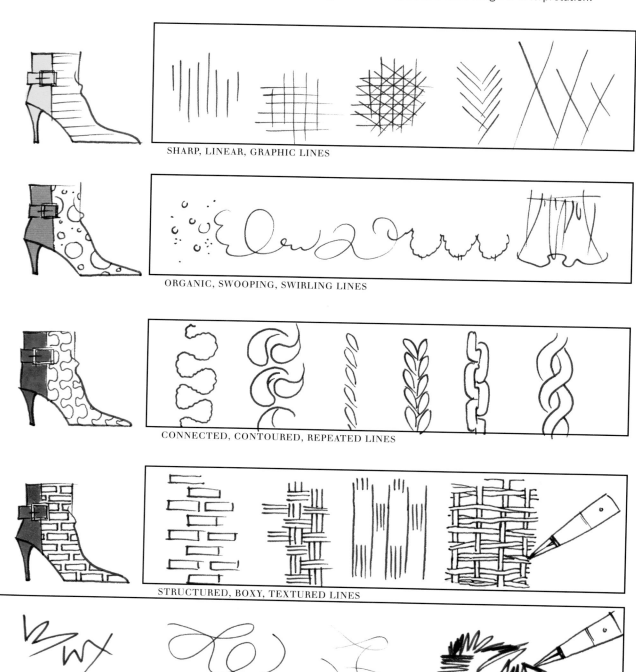

SHARP, LINEAR, GRAPHIC LINES

ORGANIC, SWOOPING, SWIRLING LINES

CONNECTED, CONTOURED, REPEATED LINES

STRUCTURED, BOXY, TEXTURED LINES

SHARP   ROUNDED   SLICED   JAGGED

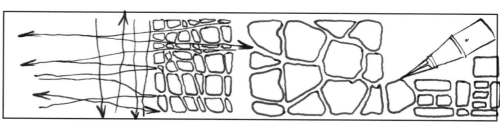

FAUX LIZARD MORFING INTO MASONRY

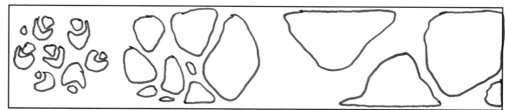

FAUX LEOPARD TURNING INTO GIRAFFE OR PONY

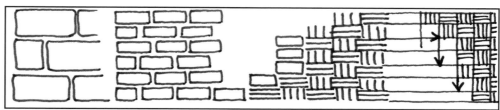

MASONRY BRICKWORK MORFING INTO BASKET WEAVE

FAUX OSTRICH TURNING INTO GRANITE, WOOD GRAIN, AND HERRINGBONE

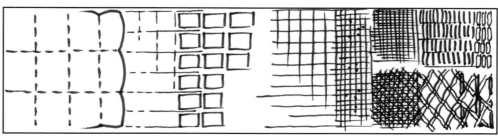

BOXED OR CHANNEL QUILTING MORFING INTO TILE WORK OR TWEEDY WEAVES

CURLY　　　　　DASHED　　　　　CHOPPY　　　　　FRINGE

Line Content

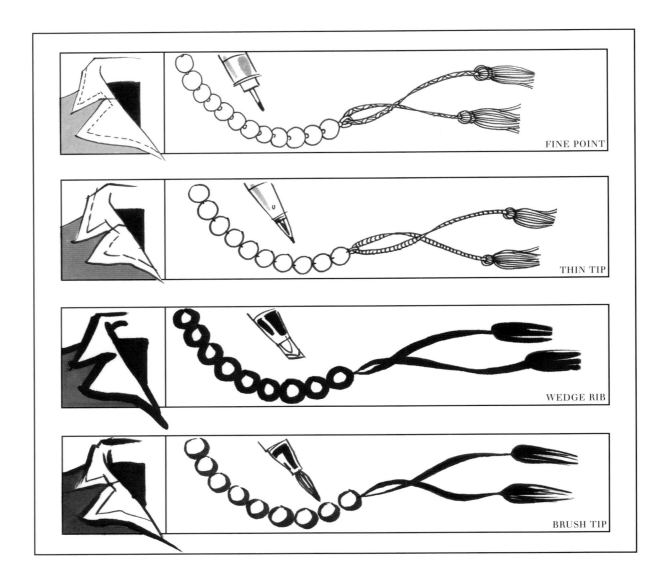

FINE POINT

THIN TIP

WEDGE RIB

BRUSH TIP

As line becomes more specific, definition and style merge to create particular images. The line, both interior and exterior, can become intricate, textured, heavy, or expressive to suit the mood, message, or attitude in your sketch. It is something you do on purpose to create the mood or look or to explain a concept in a design. Again, you pick the right tool for the task to get your message across to whoever has to "read" your sketch.

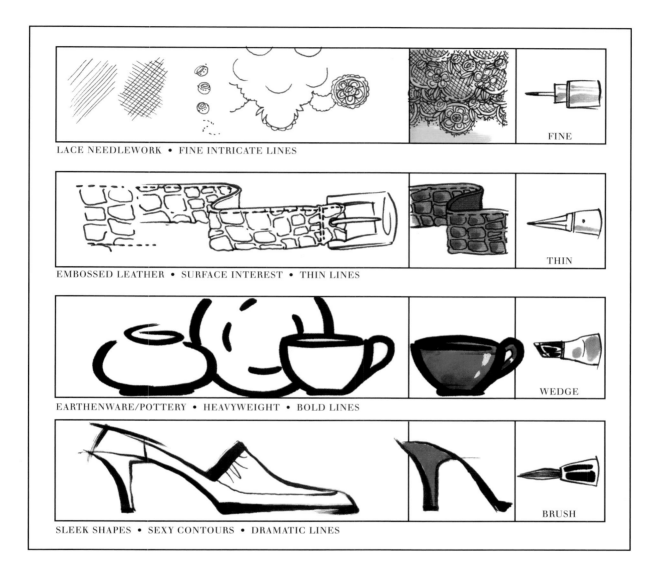

LACE NEEDLEWORK • FINE INTRICATE LINES

FINE

EMBOSSED LEATHER • SURFACE INTEREST • THIN LINES

THIN

EARTHENWARE/POTTERY • HEAVYWEIGHT • BOLD LINES

WEDGE

SLEEK SHAPES • SEXY CONTOURS • DRAMATIC LINES

BRUSH

- **Lace needlework:** Delicate, fine line for a tight, intricate, dense pattern. Areas of cross-hatching done with a .005 point.
- **Embossed leathers:** Thin line for surface interest and variety in line quality and meaning. Heavier outline; thinner interior patterning.
- **Earthenware/pottery:** Heavyweight, bulky line for suggested thickness or weight. Emphasis on size and volume in the object.
- **Silky fabric or sleek shapes:** Expressive line for mood or attitude. Focus on shape. Flexibility in line adds drama to image.

Colored Pencils with Markers

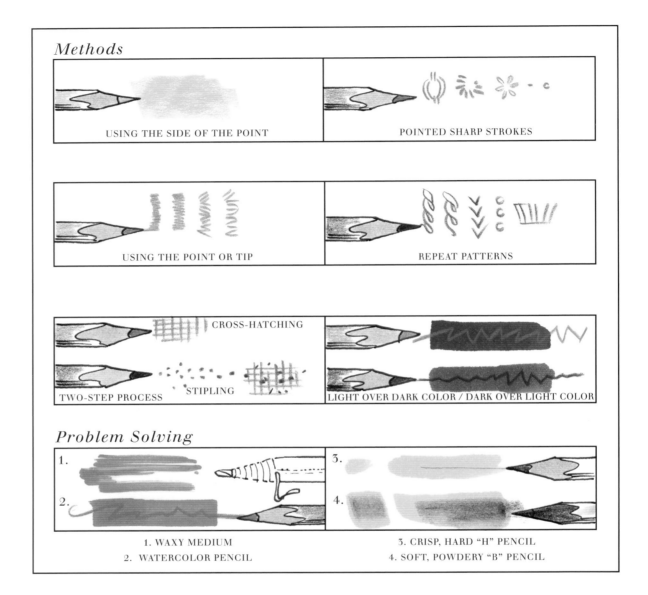

Methods

USING THE SIDE OF THE POINT

POINTED SHARP STROKES

USING THE POINT OR TIP

REPEAT PATTERNS

CROSS-HATCHING

TWO-STEP PROCESS · STIPLING

LIGHT OVER DARK COLOR / DARK OVER LIGHT COLOR

Problem Solving

1.

2.

3.

4.

1. WAXY MEDIUM
2. WATERCOLOR PENCIL

3. CRISP, HARD "H" PENCIL
4. SOFT, POWDERY "B" PENCIL

A colored pencil can be used on its tip—its sharpened point. The tip is good for thin, precision detailing. Colored pencils can be used in layers over each other or over layers of marker. There are some types of waxy media with which colored pencils are not compatible. Watercolor pencils may cause problems because they might blur underneath marker application. Soft B lead pencils may run under marker. The hard H lead pencils should do well with marker.

Mixed Media Rendering

A base layer or background color is step one in multilayered rendering.

The base color in marker rendering needs a minute to dry.

THREE STEPS—CHENILLE
ONE MARKER / TWO COLORED PENCILS

THREE STEPS—VELVET
ONE MARKER / TWO COLORED PENCILS

FOUR STEPS—EMBROIDERY
TWO MARKERS / ONE COLORED PENCIL /
GEL PEN HIGHLIGHTS

FOUR STEPS—KNIT
TWO MARKERS / ONE COLORED PENCIL
/ GEL PEN RIBBING

For most mixed media rendering, marker is the first step, or base layer, in multistep coloring techniques. The examples on this page illustrate, in various layers, textured surfaces (fabrication) that need colored pencil to complete their look. Chenille has fuzzy rows; velvet, the luxe nap; embroidery, the patterned stitches; and knits, the raised patterns. These rendering techniques take from three to four steps for each type of surface. Once you have matched the fabric's colors to your markers and pencils, one pillow can take you less than 10 minutes to complete.

Metallic Markers, Pencils, and Pens

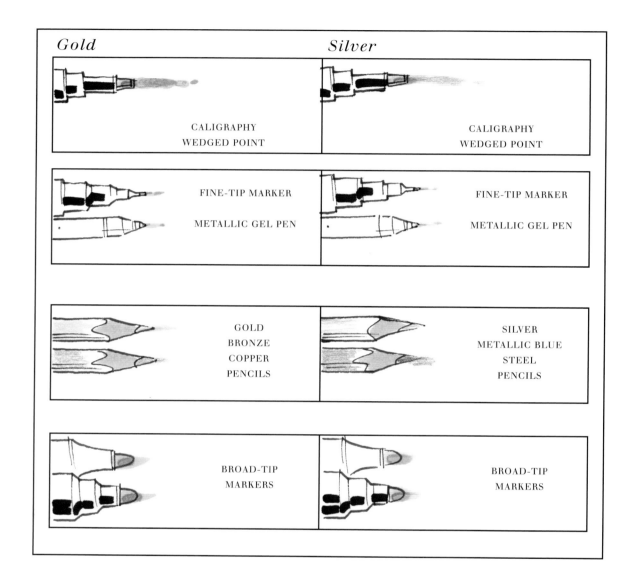

Gold   *Silver*

CALIGRAPHY WEDGED POINT   CALIGRAPHY WEDGED POINT

FINE-TIP MARKER / METALLIC GEL PEN   FINE-TIP MARKER / METALLIC GEL PEN

GOLD BRONZE COPPER PENCILS   SILVER METALLIC BLUE STEEL PENCILS

BROAD-TIP MARKERS   BROAD-TIP MARKERS

Every marker company or brand has its own version of metallic golds and silvers in thick or thin tips. At this point almost every brand uses the same ink mix and delivery system— "shake before use." One word of caution: Most markers have the potential to splatter or leave a blob when pressed too hard on the page. The colors are too valuable to abandon. So have a test sheet for practice near your art page, and shake the pens or markers away from your paper. This is another reason practice and experience with your media choices are important in your list of skills. Use these media mixes to render lamé fabrics and metallic laces.

Using Same Media for Yarn or Metal

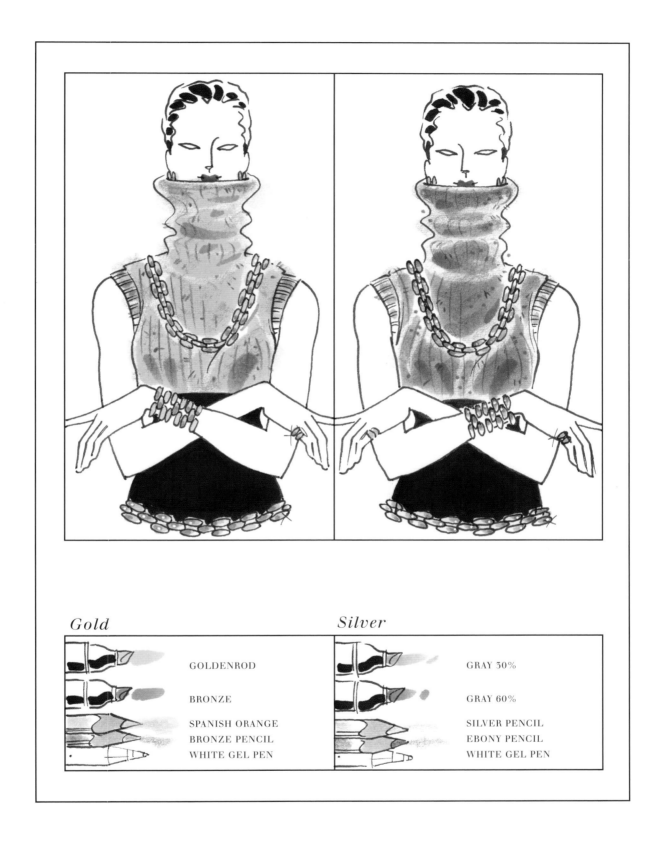

Gold

	GOLDENROD
	BRONZE
	SPANISH ORANGE
	BRONZE PENCIL
	WHITE GEL PEN

Silver

	GRAY 30%
	GRAY 60%
	SILVER PENCIL
	EBONY PENCIL
	WHITE GEL PEN

Rendering Methods

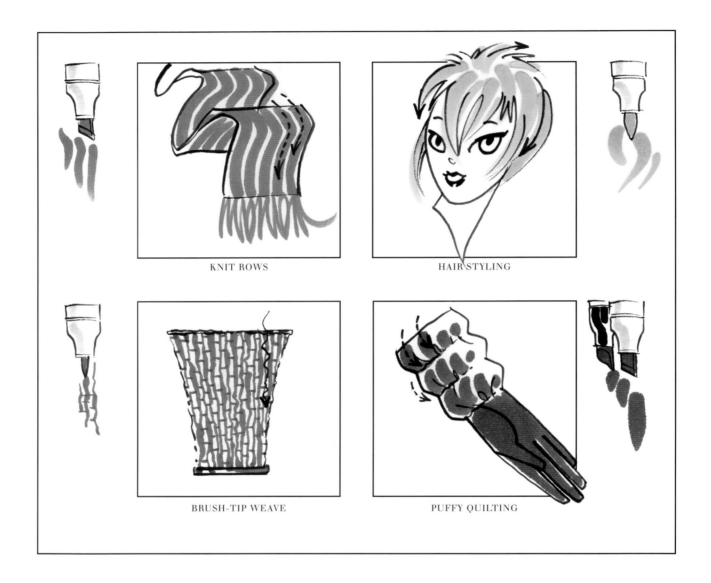

KNIT ROWS

HAIR STYLING

BRUSH-TIP WEAVE

PUFFY QUILTING

Rendering methods can be specific to a surface type or marker tip, or they may be selected for the type of coverage needed to complete a rendering. For example:

- Wedge tip for uniform but not rigid rows
- Brush tip that can easily follow contours
- Finer brush tip for undulating, open-weave coloring
- Contoured nib or wedge for mixed-rendering techniques
- Directional color that conforms to cut, drape, or construction detail
- Tight, smooth, flat coloring for all flesh tones
- Coloring in sections to control the volume of color
- Creation of two types of renderings to accommodate surface changes

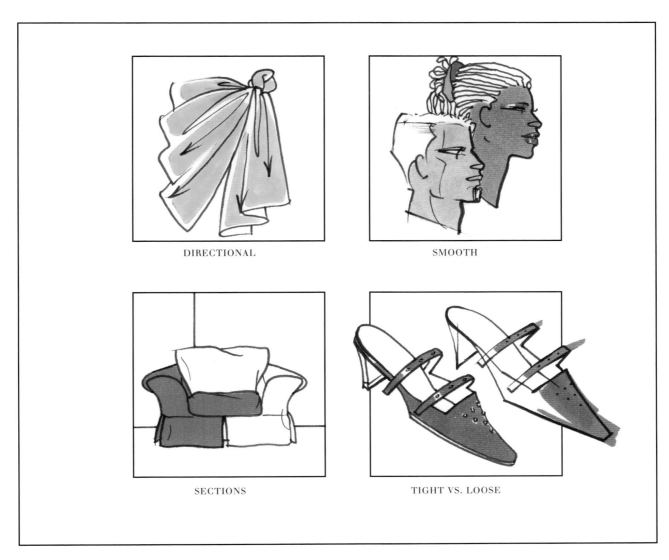

DIRECTIONAL

SMOOTH

SECTIONS

TIGHT VS. LOOSE

UNEVEN STROKES

SCRUB ACTION

SHORT DABS

DIRECTIONAL STROKES

Partial or Loose Rendering and Tight Rendering

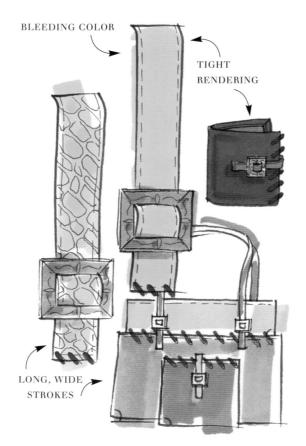

BLEEDING COLOR

TIGHT RENDERING

LONG, WIDE STROKES

Loose rendering provides minimum control. It is for a fast, rough sketch such as a (preliminary) croquis, or it's done as a stylistic preference. Either way, it's a method of minimum control done in quick, wide strokes regardless of outline contour. Loose rendering needs to be consistently done on all items within a layout to complete its look.

Tight rendering provides maximum control and is for a completed, finished sketch. It is about maximum control with a polished look. It's done with color blending or in the scrubbing technique to control the volume of color. This is where the term *bleeding* applies. That's when the color runs (accidentally) past the outline edge.

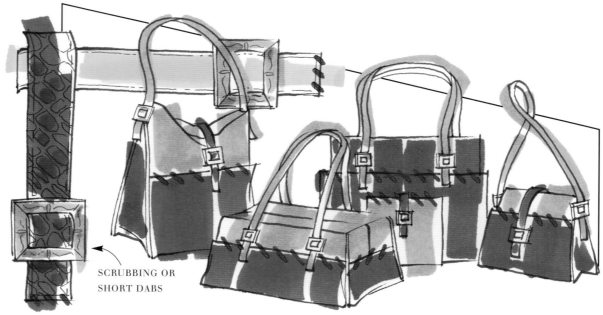

SCRUBBING OR SHORT DABS

Loose rendering for accessories or clothes looks best when it is used to accentuate shape or emphasize construction details.

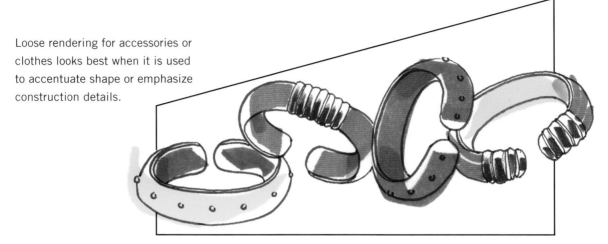

LOOSE COLOR FOR RETRO, CLASSIC, OR TRENDY PIECES

STYLE, CUT, OR SHAPE IN FORM

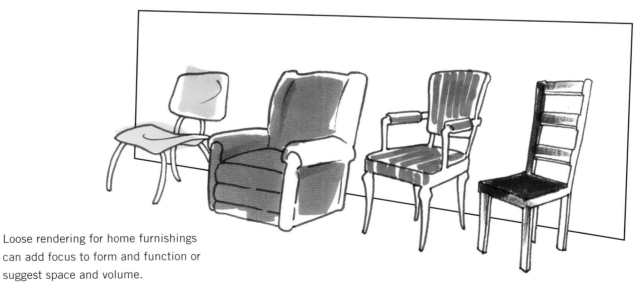

Loose rendering for home furnishings can add focus to form and function or suggest space and volume.

PLASTIC, FABRIC, OR METAL IN PARTIAL COLOR

Tight Rendering

Tight rendering is edge to edge, completed color. If a loose-color sketch is considered preliminary, then a tight sketch is called the "finish."

Tight rendering can be done in one or more coats. You can start in the middle or at the edge. It doesn't matter as long as the coloring is even and precise and does not obscure the details or bleed past the the outline contour of the item.

Note that there are at least four different methods (see page 21) to practice to hone your skills for tight rendering.

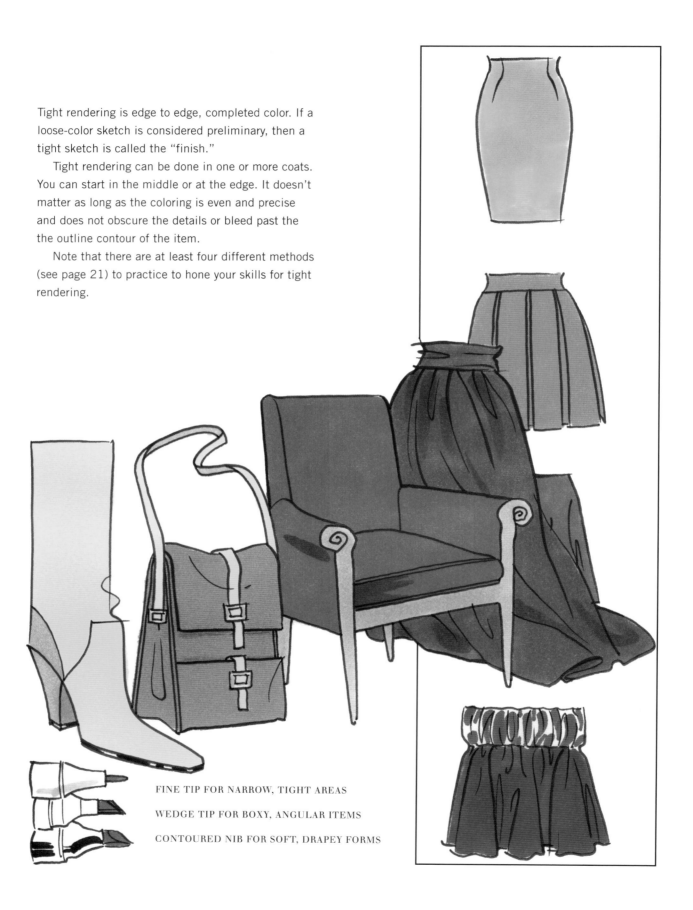

FINE TIP FOR NARROW, TIGHT AREAS

WEDGE TIP FOR BOXY, ANGULAR ITEMS

CONTOURED NIB FOR SOFT, DRAPEY FORMS

Techniques for Tight Rendering

SCRUBBING AND BLENDING

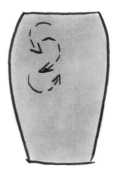

TIGHT RENDERING

Scrubbing and Blending

Use the tip of the marker to drag the color back and forth over itself to keep the color wet as you apply it. This cuts down on color streaking.

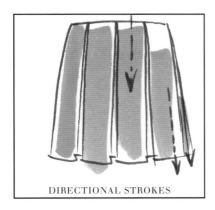

DIRECTIONAL STROKES

TIGHT RENDERING

Directional Strokes

Work in a direction—top to bottom or up and down—because this type of coloring will complement the construction or shape of the item.

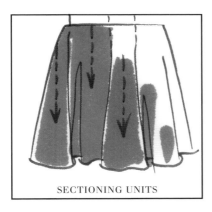

SECTIONING UNITS

TIGHT RENDERING

Sectioning Units

This kind of coloring divides the shape into sections. You look for natural breaks or units to control the amount of color that you work with at one time.

COMBINED / MIXED

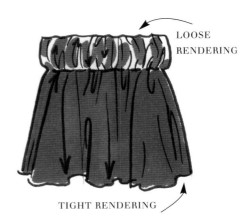

LOOSE RENDERING

TIGHT RENDERING

Combined / Mixed

Sometimes you have to emphasize one part of a sketch as different from another part. For this type of rendering you can combine techniques as a visual device to emphasize these differences.

Tight Versus Loose Rendering

Tight versus loose, or partial, rendering is the artist's choice. Sometimes it's about stylistic preference—liking one look better than the other—regardless of size or presentation issues. It helps to color one set of images in both styles of rendering to get familiar with the differences between them. Decide what is too little or too much color. When it comes to fashion figures, loose rendering can look as good as tight on flesh tones as long as the rendering of the flesh tones is consistent with rendering of the clothes, with or without the use of a light source.

Finished or Tight Rendering

SOLIDS: SHADED LOOK ACCORDING TO CONSTRUCTION OR LIGHT SOURCE

PRINTS: SHADED FIRST TO AVOID STREAKING OF PRINTS' COLORS

FINISHED OR TIGHT
RENDERING ON FLESH TONE

Loose or Partial Rendering

LOOSE OR PARTIAL
RENDERING ON
FLESH TONE

Solid Color: Options

1. Spill color down the center toward the hemline.
2. Use a light source side for color placement.

Prints: Options

1. Spill the print down the middle.
2. Use a light source direction.

Fabric Rendering

Rendering patterns based on simple lines or a grid is a great way to learn how to handle a print. For these, you can plan the patterns using a light 4-H pencil that disappears under the marker. Working out prints like these will give you the skills you'll need to deal with more complex fabrics. Note that real animal skins and furs are rendered the same way as faux, or fake, skins and furs.

MARKER, PENCIL, AND PEN MIX

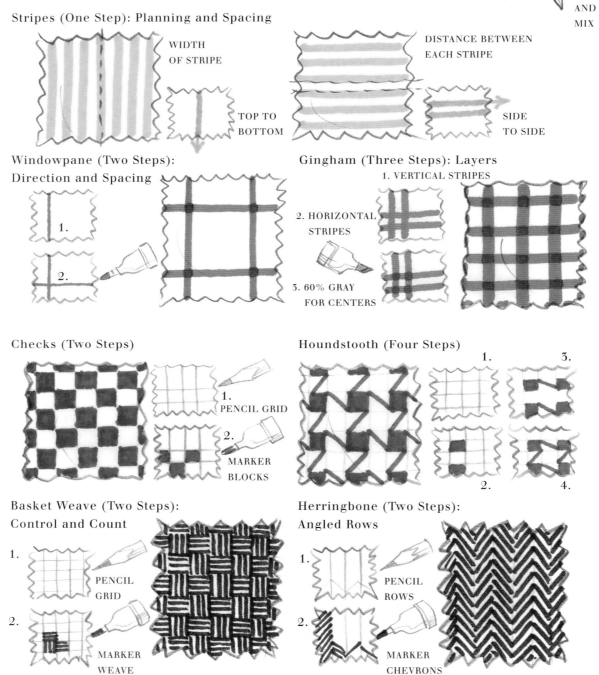

Stripes (One Step): Planning and Spacing

WIDTH OF STRIPE

TOP TO BOTTOM

DISTANCE BETWEEN EACH STRIPE

SIDE TO SIDE

Windowpane (Two Steps): Direction and Spacing

1.

2.

Gingham (Three Steps): Layers

1. VERTICAL STRIPES

2. HORIZONTAL STRIPES

3. 60% GRAY FOR CENTERS

Checks (Two Steps)

1. PENCIL GRID

2. MARKER BLOCKS

Houndstooth (Four Steps)

1. 2. 3. 4.

Basket Weave (Two Steps): Control and Count

1. PENCIL GRID

2. MARKER WEAVE

Herringbone (Two Steps): Angled Rows

1. PENCIL ROWS

2. MARKER CHEVRONS

The examples on this page illustrate the correlation between some fabrics that have overlapping rendering techniques, plus or minus a few layers. You can save time by adapting relating prep work or coloring methods from simple fabrics to more complex, difficult ones.

Stripes Turning into Corduroy

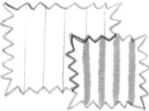

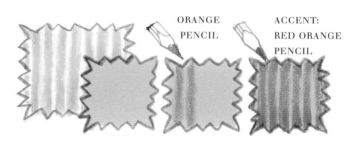

ORANGE PENCIL

ACCENT: RED ORANGE PENCIL

Gingham Turning into Basic Plaid

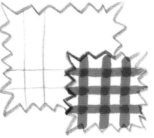
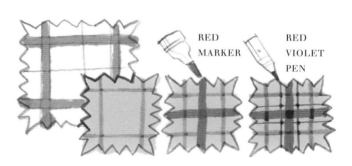

RED MARKER

RED VIOLET PEN

Checks Turning into Polka Dots Turning into Petite Floral

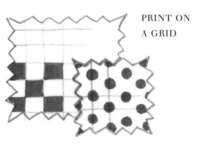

PRINT ON A GRID

ORANGE PEN GRID

RED AND VIOLET PEN

Linear Prints Turning into Textures

Colored pencil overlays: 2 or 3 steps

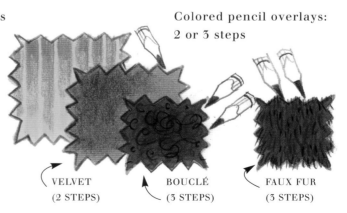

VELVET (2 STEPS)

BOUCLÉ (3 STEPS)

FAUX FUR (3 STEPS)

Details in Rendering

Pen and Brush Pen

Fringe: Short strokes in angular motions. Work from where the fringe is sewn in (seamed), brushing out to the length of it, adding a bit of flare or flip in the row.

Embroidery: Extra short, abbreviated lines. You can start in the middle of the shape and "stitch" your way out or weave the rows together.

Edging: With the many options in edging, tailor your line to its construction points; fill-in, slant, or zigzag versus straight lines. Just control the width.

Lace and Crochet: Fragile-looking, delicate lines. Start with the edges and work your way into the rows or repeat pattern. Fill in the connecting web of lines last.

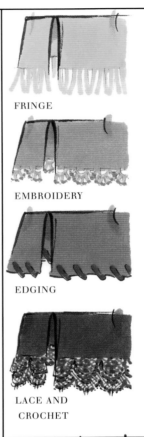

FRINGE

EMBROIDERY

EDGING

LACE AND
CROCHET

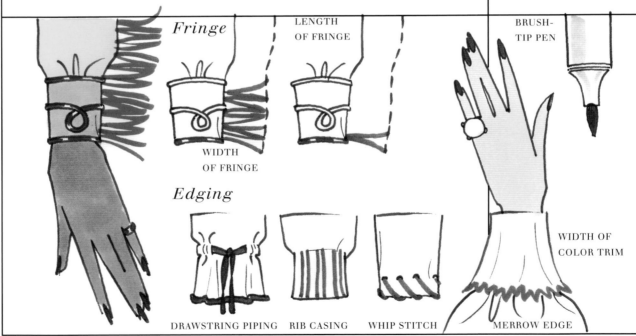

Fringe

LENGTH
OF FRINGE

WIDTH
OF FRINGE

Edging

DRAWSTRING PIPING   RIB CASING   WHIP STITCH   MERROW EDGE

BRUSH-
TIP PEN

WIDTH OF
COLOR TRIM

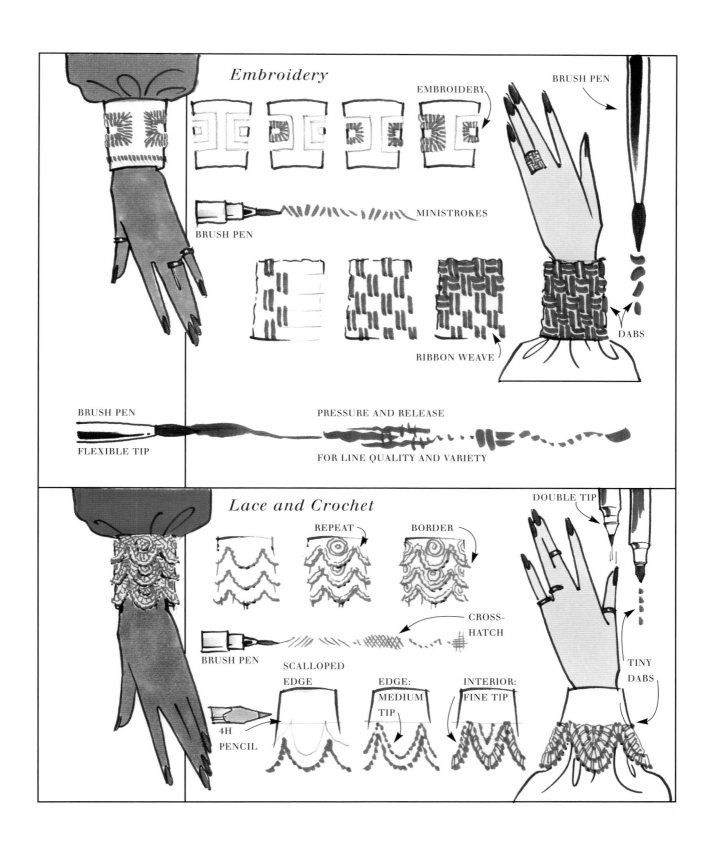

Embroidery

EMBROIDERY

BRUSH PEN

BRUSH PEN

MINISTROKES

RIBBON WEAVE

DABS

BRUSH PEN

PRESSURE AND RELEASE

FLEXIBLE TIP

FOR LINE QUALITY AND VARIETY

Lace and Crochet

DOUBLE TIP

REPEAT

BORDER

CROSS-HATCH

BRUSH PEN

SCALLOPED EDGE

EDGE: MEDIUM TIP

INTERIOR: FINE TIP

TINY DABS

4H PENCIL

Assignment

This assignment will enable you to discover the options for line in a variety of pens or markers. Test the differences between a brush pen, a calligraphy tipped pen, and a regular pen that can have a wide, medium, or fine point. Investigate the results of thicker, thinner, and striated lines. First, analyze the types of lines that these pens or markers create. Second, evaluate how to apply various lines and teach yourself control over these implements.

Block out four small boxes. Each box will have its own set of lines, each different from the other. You are in control of these differences.

- **First Box:** Make light, thin, pale lines.
- **Second Box:** Create ragged, angular, sharp lines.
- **Third Box:** Draw bold, heavy, dark lines.
- **Fourth Box:** Make organic, rounded, curvy lines.

Next make four new boxes. Fill these in with bits of repeat line gleaned from the first set of four boxes, creating four different patterns. All eight boxes are about results. Did you get what you wanted, and do you like what you did?

CHAPTER 2

RENDERING

SOLID COLORS

Checklist for Rendering Solid Colors

Paper

Some papers have a right (front) and wrong (back) side, and both sides do not always "take" marker in the same way. Sometimes the back of a piece of paper is a problem and does not accept marker color. Remember which is the front, or right side, of a paper when you tear it out of a pad.

If you do not remove the paper from the pad, always use a slipsheet, a shield, or a sheet of loose paper between the top sheet and the paper underneath it. This will protect your working surface from bleeding—color that runs onto and ruins the paper underneath.

Markers

Test a marker before you use it on your sketch. Use test strips to determine whether a marker is too wet or too dry.

Make sure you hear the snap or click of your marker caps when you close them to ensure that the cover is on tight.

Pencils

Use an H pencil (4H or 6H hard leads) for pencil sketching before rendering. Soft leads (the Bs) will smudge under marker.

Use a 4H or 6H pencil for an under-sketch or preliminary drawing on a shape that you plan to color. Hard leads produce light lines that usually disappear under the marker color.

Pencil as an outline or edge of your marker rendering is done last. Use any type of pencil desired. Again, wait for the marker drawing to dry before you pencil over it.

Watercolor pencils can bleed or run under markers.

Pens

If you apply a pen line as an outline holding line around the color after you have finished with your markers, make sure the marker colors are set or dry—that's approximately a two- or three-minute wait between layers.

Check your pen with your markers on a test sheet to ensure that it does not run or bleed into the marker coloring process.

Test Page

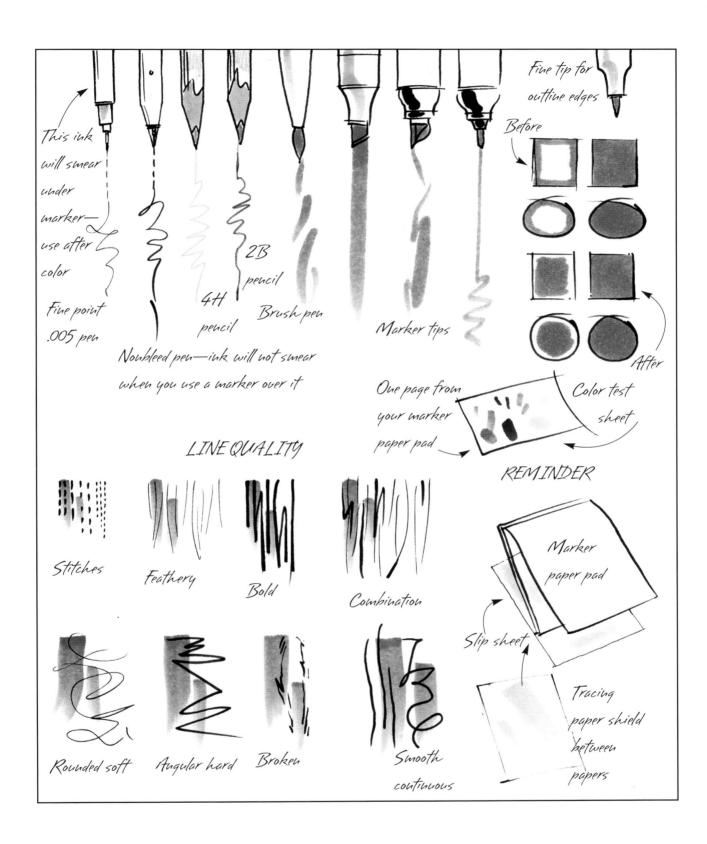

This ink will smear under marker—use after color

Fine point .005 pen

4H pencil

2B pencil

Noubleed pen—ink will not smear when you use a marker over it

Brush pen

Marker tips

Fine tip for outline edges

Before

After

One page from your marker paper pad

Color test sheet

REMINDER

LINE QUALITY

Stitches

Feathery

Bold

Combination

Rounded soft

Angular hard

Broken

Smooth continuous

Marker paper pad

Slip sheet

Tracing paper shield between papers

Review

The scrub rendering technique shown earlier does not have to be for tight coloring only. You can also use it for loose rendering. Notice how loose coloring emphasizes the chunky angularity in the box pleat.

Loose

You can learn to control loose rendering to make it accentuate nuance, detail, or construction in a shape. Look how loose strokes of color focus on the size of the side pleats here.

Tight

Tight rendering may be necessary when you want to add shading to make some detail deeper, fuller, or more dramatic. For gathered materials loose rendering can look too choppy if you're not careful.

Mixed

There are always rule breakers. Novelty treatments or fabrics need either a mix of rendering treatments or a hybrid of both loose and tight rendering in the form of the detail or construction itself. Notice how the mushroom and accordion pleating dictate the application of color here.

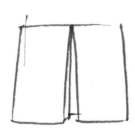

BOX PLEAT

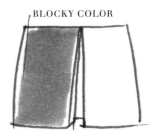

BLOCKY COLOR

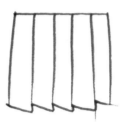

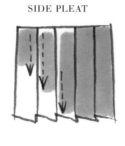

SIDE PLEAT

SINGLE STROKES

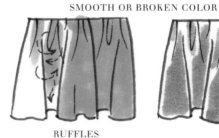

SMOOTH OR BROKEN COLOR

RUFFLES

SQUIGGLE COLOR

RULE-BREAKING COLOR

MUSHROOM PLEATS

ACCORDION PLEATS

LOOSE   MIXED   TIGHT

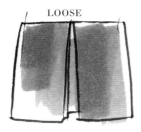  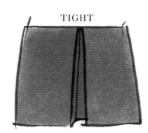

RENDERING STYLES
APPLY TO ALL NIBS EXCEPT
FOR THE FINE POINTS

LOOSE   MIXED   TIGHT

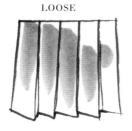  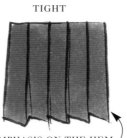

PLEATS PUT THE EMPHASIS ON THE HEM

GATHERS PUT THE EMPHASIS ON THE SEAM

LOOSE   MIXED   TIGHT

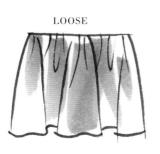  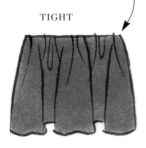

MIXED   MIXED

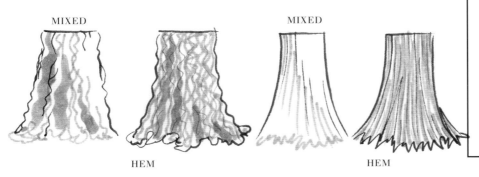

HEM   HEM

This page and the page opposite illustrate some of the options in solid color rendering. This kind of rendering is basic but not boring if you use it to feature a particular aspect in the design such as the angles in a pleat or the gathers in a ruffle. You should practice this kind of rendering. Working on a page like this would help you with new rendering challenges and would familiarize you with too much, too little, or just the right amount of marker coloring. Make sure to practice using different marker nibs to get used to the plus and minus factors in each construction type.

Solid Colors for Interior Design

Drawing an object with (or without) the benefit of per-spective does not dictate your coloring technique. Solid, flat color can be applied to solitary items or to the room or layout. Color in the direction of the walls rather than the floor or its covering in order to get any streaking factor to work to your advantage as the streaks carry your eye across the sketch. Color in units or sections of an item. Change your coloring technique when you introduce a new surface.

COLOR HORIZONTALLY FOR THE FLOOR

BRUSH AND WEDGE NIBS
ARE FINE FOR SHORT STROKES
OR SMALL DABS

SCRUB THE COLOR OR WORK IN SECTIONS

COLOR VERTICALLY FOR THE WALLS

DIRECTIONAL COLORING METHOD
FOR DRAPERIES

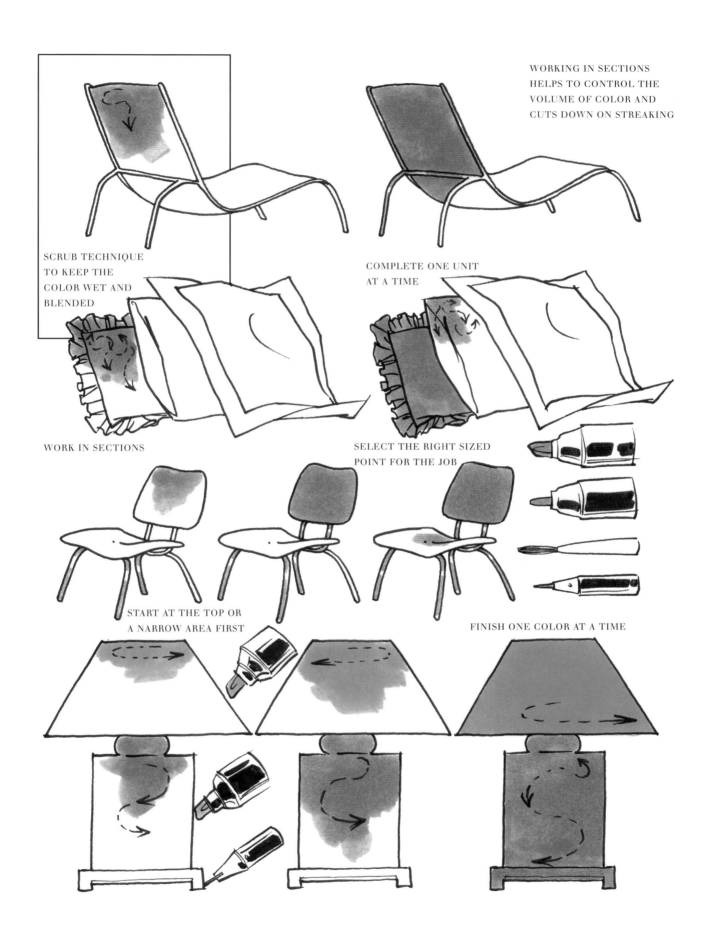

WORKING IN SECTIONS
HELPS TO CONTROL THE
VOLUME OF COLOR AND
CUTS DOWN ON STREAKING

SCRUB TECHNIQUE
TO KEEP THE
COLOR WET AND
BLENDED

COMPLETE ONE UNIT
AT A TIME

WORK IN SECTIONS

SELECT THE RIGHT SIZED
POINT FOR THE JOB

START AT THE TOP OR
A NARROW AREA FIRST

FINISH ONE COLOR AT A TIME

Solid Color Rendering for Accessories

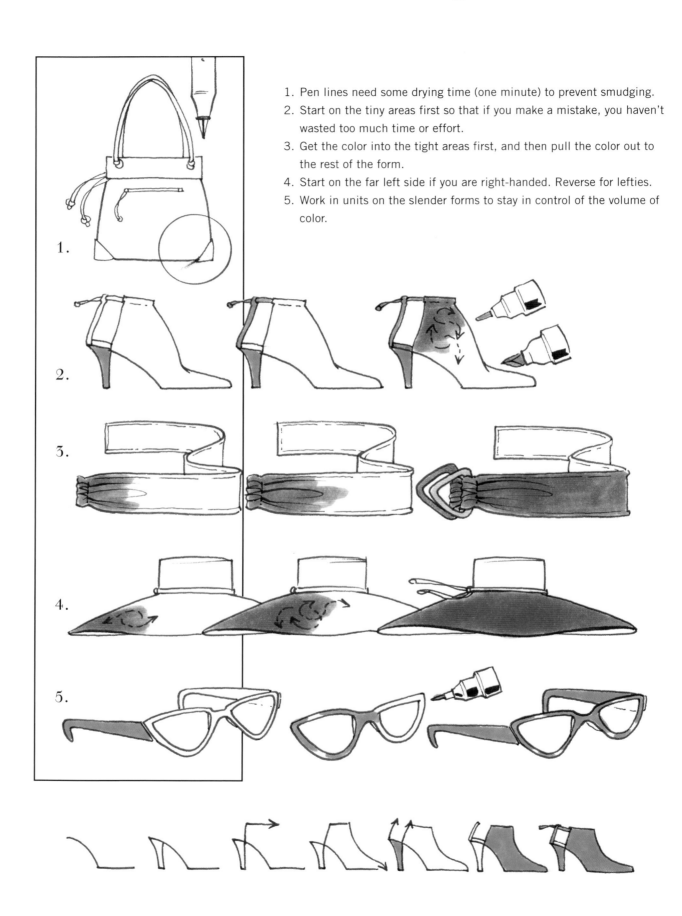

1. Pen lines need some drying time (one minute) to prevent smudging.
2. Start on the tiny areas first so that if you make a mistake, you haven't wasted too much time or effort.
3. Get the color into the tight areas first, and then pull the color out to the rest of the form.
4. Start on the far left side if you are right-handed. Reverse for lefties.
5. Work in units on the slender forms to stay in control of the volume of color.

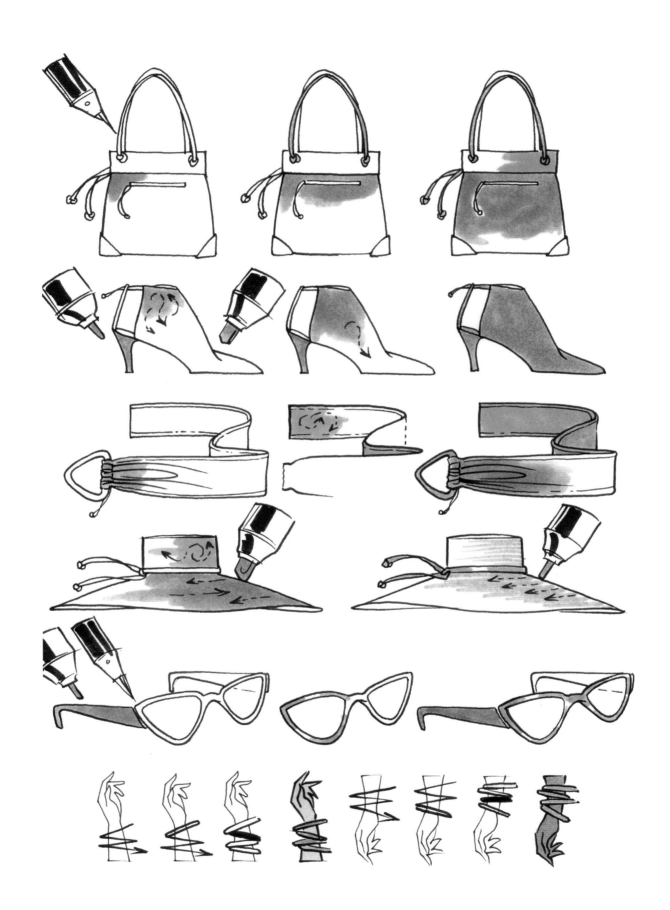

Solid Color Rendering for Fashion

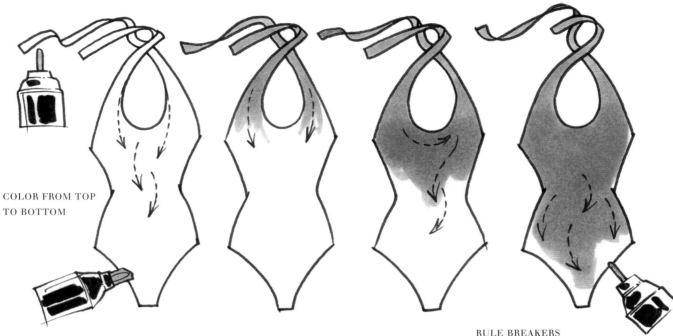

COLOR FROM TOP
TO BOTTOM

Basic Scrub Technique

One of the simplest coloring methods is to begin at the top of the form and drag the color down to the bottom. This works well with a flat. On the opposite page is another flat that presents the challenge of drape. You should color the drape to accentuate the pull or direction in the fabric. So you color from side to side instead of from top to bottom. Either way, you can still use the scrub technique to smooth out the color across the garment.

RULE BREAKERS

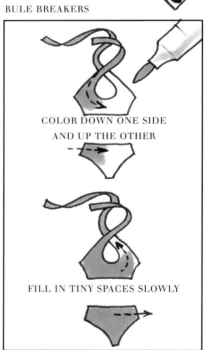

COLOR DOWN ONE SIDE
AND UP THE OTHER

FILL IN TINY SPACES SLOWLY

BUILD THE TORSO TO CONTROL THE
SIZE OF THE FLATS

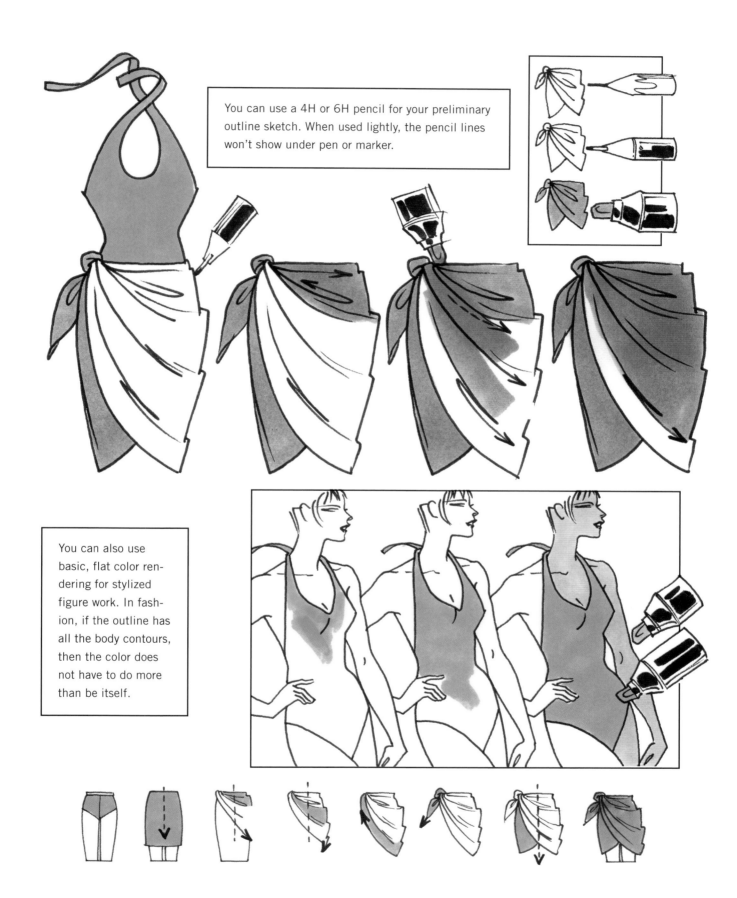

You can use a 4H or 6H pencil for your preliminary outline sketch. When used lightly, the pencil lines won't show under pen or marker.

You can also use basic, flat color rendering for stylized figure work. In fashion, if the outline has all the body contours, then the color does not have to do more than be itself.

Solid Color Flesh Tones

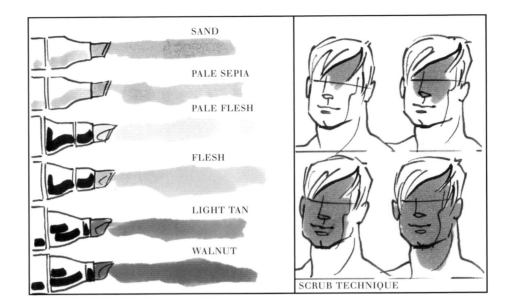

SAND

PALE SEPIA

PALE FLESH

FLESH

LIGHT TAN

WALNUT

SCRUB TECHNIQUE

Markers have a fabulous range of flesh tones from deep, golden browns to pale, barely there beiges. Every race is represented in this broad spectrum of flesh tones—in all brands of markers—in all types of nibs.

The flesh tones used for the men on this page have a slightly cool, olive cast to them. On the opposite page, for women, the flesh tone colors have a slightly warmer, peachy cast. As you can see, all the colors look great together.

WORKING IN LAYERS

| EGGSHELL OR BUFF | BRICK BEIGE OR LIGHT SAND | SEPIA OR DESERT TAN | BURNT UMBER OR MOCHA | LIGHT TAN IN TWO LAYERS |

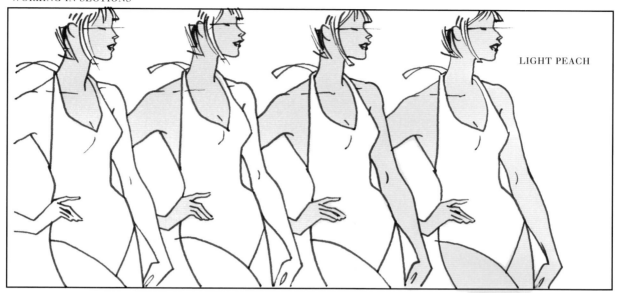

LIGHT PEACH

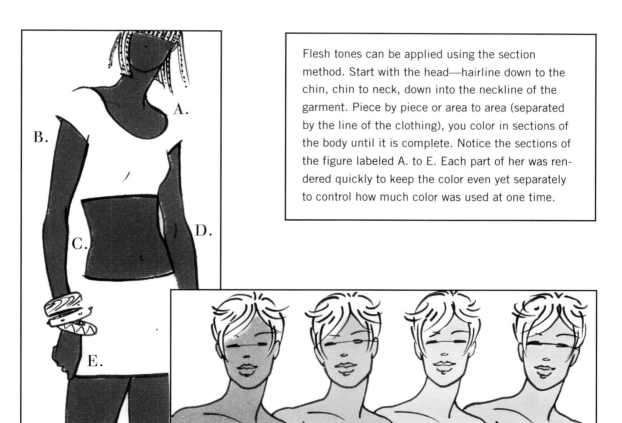

B.

A.

C.

D.

E.

Flesh tones can be applied using the section method. Start with the head—hairline down to the chin, chin to neck, down into the neckline of the garment. Piece by piece or area to area (separated by the line of the clothing), you color in sections of the body until it is complete. Notice the sections of the figure labeled A. to E. Each part of her was rendered quickly to keep the color even yet separately to control how much color was used at one time.

REDWOOD   PALE CHERRY   FLESH   SUNSET PINK   LIGHT PEACH

Full Figure Rendering

Shirtless or Bare Upper Torso

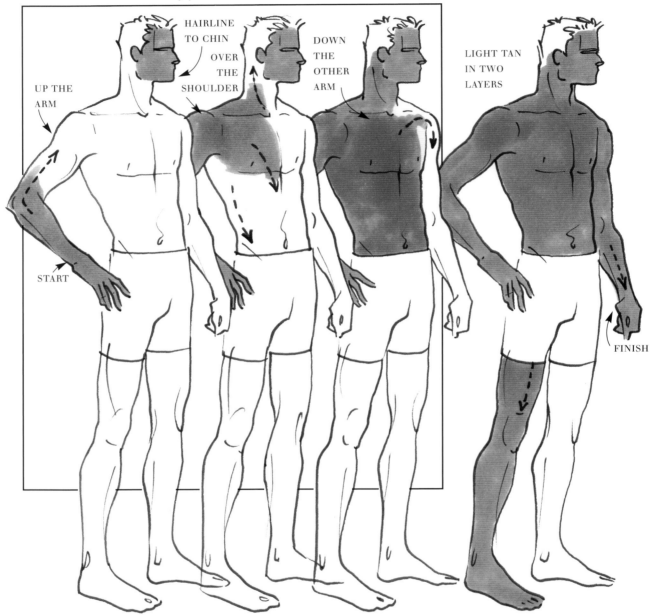

One of the more difficult situations in flesh tone rendering is when the arms and upper torso are bare—shirtless for menswear or strapless for womenswear. It is difficult because you have to color a long, extended area of the body while avoiding streaks or uneven coloring. The solution to this problem is on this page and the page opposite. Start with one hand or arm, work up to the shoulder, across the chest or upper torso, over and down to the other arm, finishing at the other hand and opposite to where you began. Page 45 illustrates more coloring via sections, which gives you more control over the coloring process.

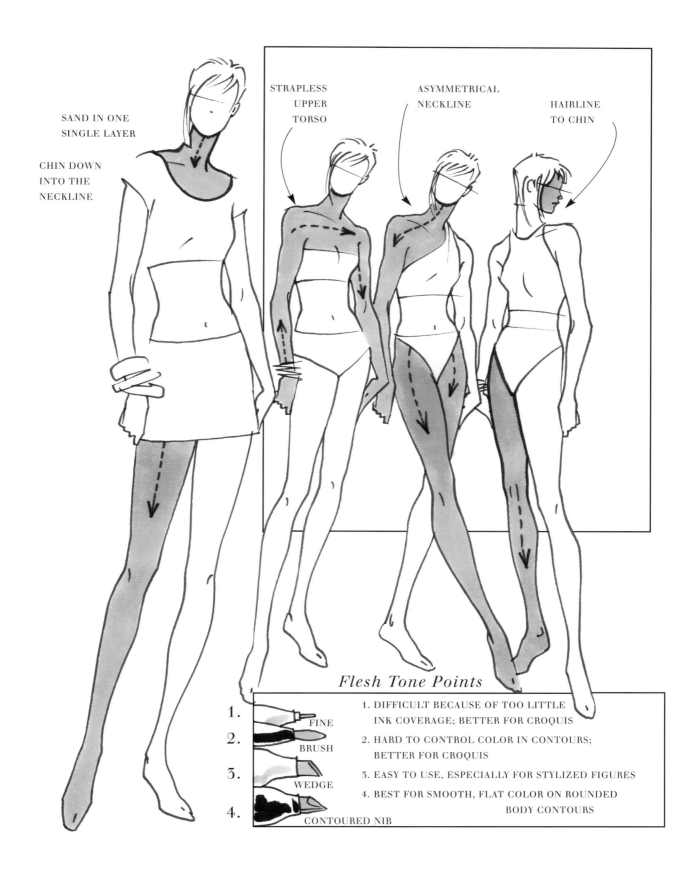

SAND IN ONE
SINGLE LAYER

CHIN DOWN
INTO THE
NECKLINE

STRAPLESS
UPPER
TORSO

ASYMMETRICAL
NECKLINE

HAIRLINE
TO CHIN

Flesh Tone Points

1. FINE

2. BRUSH

3. WEDGE

4. CONTOURED NIB

1. DIFFICULT BECAUSE OF TOO LITTLE
   INK COVERAGE; BETTER FOR CROQUIS

2. HARD TO CONTROL COLOR IN CONTOURS;
   BETTER FOR CROQUIS

3. EASY TO USE, ESPECIALLY FOR STYLIZED FIGURES

4. BEST FOR SMOOTH, FLAT COLOR ON ROUNDED
   BODY CONTOURS

Flesh Tone for Croquis

Do the pen line first to make sure that it won't smudge under marker coloring. Let the pen line dry two minutes before you begin coloring.

Even colored, smooth flesh tones are accomplished by working quickly to keep the color wet as you drag it across the forms. Scrubbing mixes the color evenly to prevent streaking.

To control streaking, cut down on the volume of color by breaking the flesh tone areas into units. Little areas are easier to color quickly.

Start at the top of a unit or body section. Pull the color down in short dabs so that the color won't run or bleed.

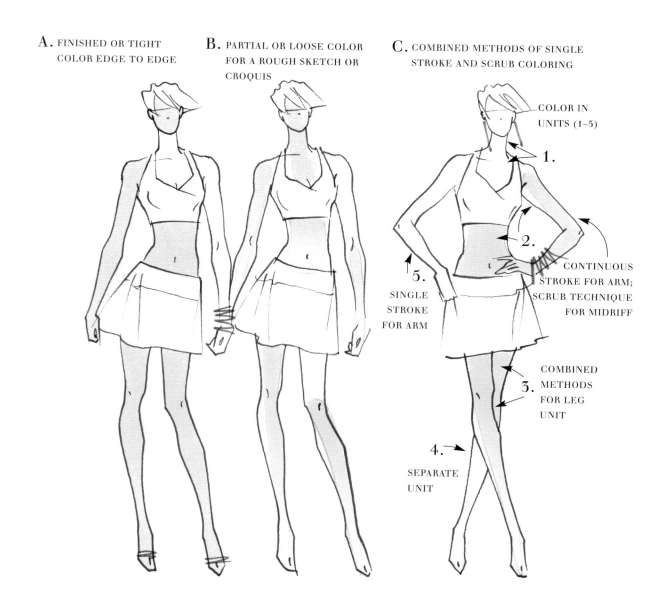

A. FINISHED OR TIGHT COLOR EDGE TO EDGE

B. PARTIAL OR LOOSE COLOR FOR A ROUGH SKETCH OR CROQUIS

C. COMBINED METHODS OF SINGLE STROKE AND SCRUB COLORING

COLOR IN UNITS (1–5)

1.

2.

5.

SINGLE STROKE FOR ARM

CONTINUOUS STROKE FOR ARM; SCRUB TECHNIQUE FOR MIDRIFF

COMBINED METHODS FOR LEG UNIT

3.

4.

SEPARATE UNIT

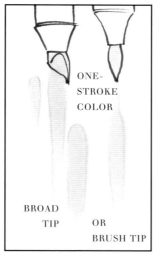

ONE-
STROKE
COLOR

BROAD
TIP   OR
         BRUSH TIP

Croquis are usually smaller figures, quick rough drawings used for working out concept and design direction. These types of preliminary sketches require partial or loose rendering. Flesh tones in croquis can be done in a brush tip or fine point. You can also use the tip of the contour nib in little dabs of color or in short, single strokes to control and define flesh tone areas on the figure.

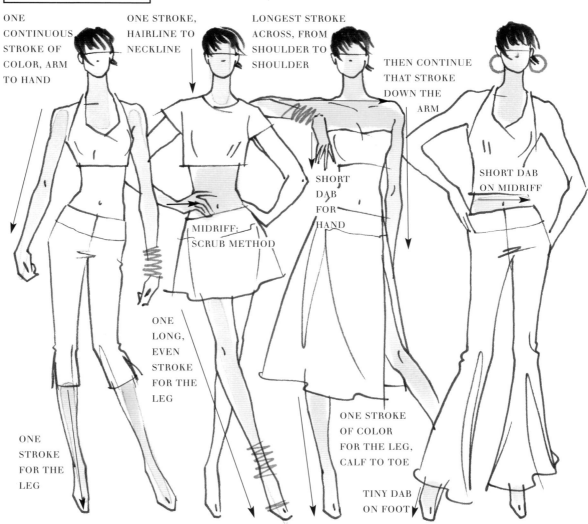

ONE
CONTINUOUS
STROKE OF
COLOR, ARM
TO HAND

ONE STROKE,
HAIRLINE TO
NECKLINE

LONGEST STROKE
ACROSS, FROM
SHOULDER TO
SHOULDER

THEN CONTINUE
THAT STROKE
DOWN THE
ARM

SHORT DAB
ON MIDRIFF

SHORT
DAB
FOR
HAND

MIDRIFF:
SCRUB METHOD

ONE
LONG,
EVEN
STROKE
FOR THE
LEG

ONE
STROKE
FOR THE
LEG

ONE STROKE
OF COLOR
FOR THE LEG,
CALF TO TOE

TINY DAB
ON FOOT

Rendering Hair

Rendering hair, as a skill, really belongs in Chapter 4, "Layered Color," but it also follows naturally from flesh tone.

Blonde
Blonde hair, beyond your choice in yellows, looks natural with golden or brown highlights.

Redhead
Red hair can be brassy and bold when you add burgundy highlights.

Brunette
For brunettes, deep brown or jet black is fine on its own with the white of the paper as highlights, or you can add blue or gray highlights as sheen.

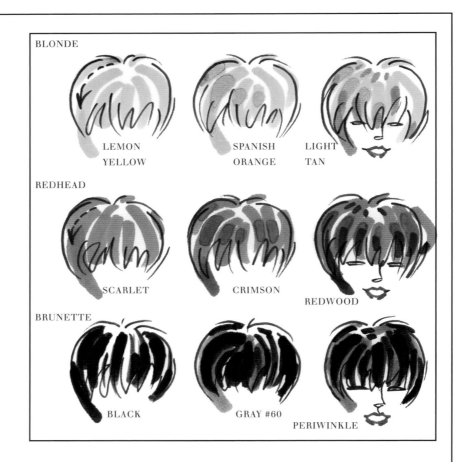

BLONDE

LEMON YELLOW — SPANISH ORANGE — LIGHT TAN

REDHEAD

SCARLET — CRIMSON — REDWOOD

BRUNETTE

BLACK — GRAY #60 — PERIWINKLE

CLASSIC — STYLIZED — ANIME

Layered Colors with Pen Line for Hair
Hair can be drawn in any shape, in any color, and in any drawing style. These are just examples to get you started. They demonstrate realistic, stylized, and cartoon-type hair renderings. Hair color works in solid, flat color. It also works in two or three layers of related colors, which give the hair density and volume—without making it look like fabric.

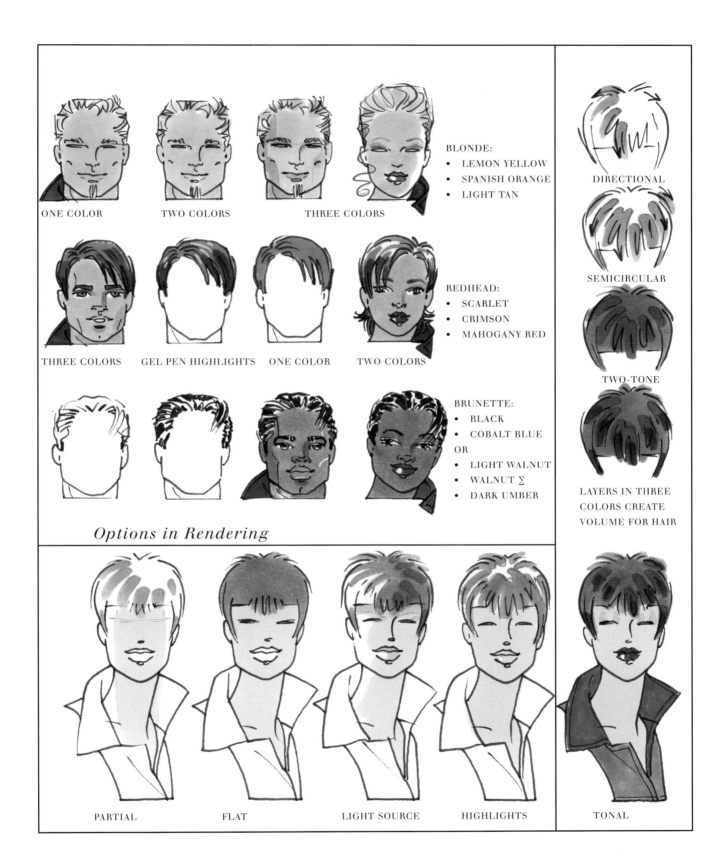

ONE COLOR   TWO COLORS   THREE COLORS

BLONDE:
- LEMON YELLOW
- SPANISH ORANGE
- LIGHT TAN

DIRECTIONAL

THREE COLORS   GEL PEN HIGHLIGHTS   ONE COLOR   TWO COLORS

REDHEAD:
- SCARLET
- CRIMSON
- MAHOGANY RED

SEMICIRCULAR

BRUNETTE:
- BLACK
- COBALT BLUE

OR
- LIGHT WALNUT
- WALNUT Σ
- DARK UMBER

TWO-TONE

LAYERS IN THREE
COLORS CREATE
VOLUME FOR HAIR

Options in Rendering

PARTIAL   FLAT   LIGHT SOURCE   HIGHLIGHTS

TONAL

Assignment

Practice on basic, single items with solid, flat color. Then color a collection of items. This could be for fashion, accessories, or interiors. The point is to render a few colors together, matching them in value and smoothness. This type of practice brings different colors edge to edge, forcing you to color very carefully next to the holding lines in your sketch. For example, see the flesh tone next to the tank top over the shorts shown below.

Sketch in 4H pencil or work directly in pen line. For fashion or accessories, your collection could be in two to four pieces, in three or four colors. For interiors, put together a room with enough elements to need three to four colors. Complete each single color before working on the next. Focusing on one color at a time helps you to keep them even. If you make a mistake, keep it, label the problem, and learn from it rather than getting rid of it.

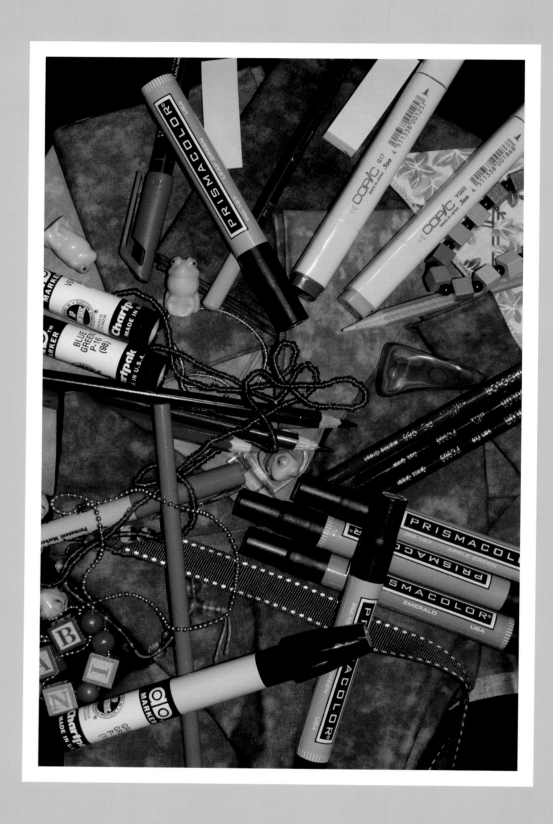

CHAPTER 3

SHADING

Checklist for Shading

Paper Marker papers are thin, lightweight, and vulnerable to creases, pressure spots, and fingerprints. Protect the edges of the paper from curling or folding by being careful as you lean on the paper to work.

Pressure spots or fingerprints happen when you use the hand you're not drawing with to anchor the page. The solution is to place a loose sheet of tracing paper under that hand. Invisible fingerprints affect the color on the page or may even prevent color from showing up there.

Always use the same type of paper in your finished sketch as you use for your demo test strip page.

Markers Shading for markers can be done in warm or cool grays. Be aware of the differences between these. Each brand has its own gray markers, and they are all different shades. Always practice on a test strip before rendering with gray markers. For example, it would not look right if you mix one brand's gray 40 percent with another company's gray 40 percent in the same sketch, because the two shades would not match.

Shading can also be done with color on color; for example, red on green or blue on orange. You should make a test strip of your base color big enough (on the demo page) to determine what colors have the right contrast to represent shading.

Only some brands of markers are compatible with others. All work together side by side but some brands, because of their chemical mix, will not blend. They run or smudge the base color. Again, always test first on your demo page.

Pencils Colored pencils are another source for shading. The challenge is to tone down their gritty nature to control the shading and make a solid shadow. Or you could play up the gritty nature of a colored pencil to add texture in combination with the shadow to emphasize the weave or surface in the base color.

Soft lead black pencils, like a 4B, appear naturally gray but be aware that these soft lead pencils tend to smear on smoother papers like marker paper.

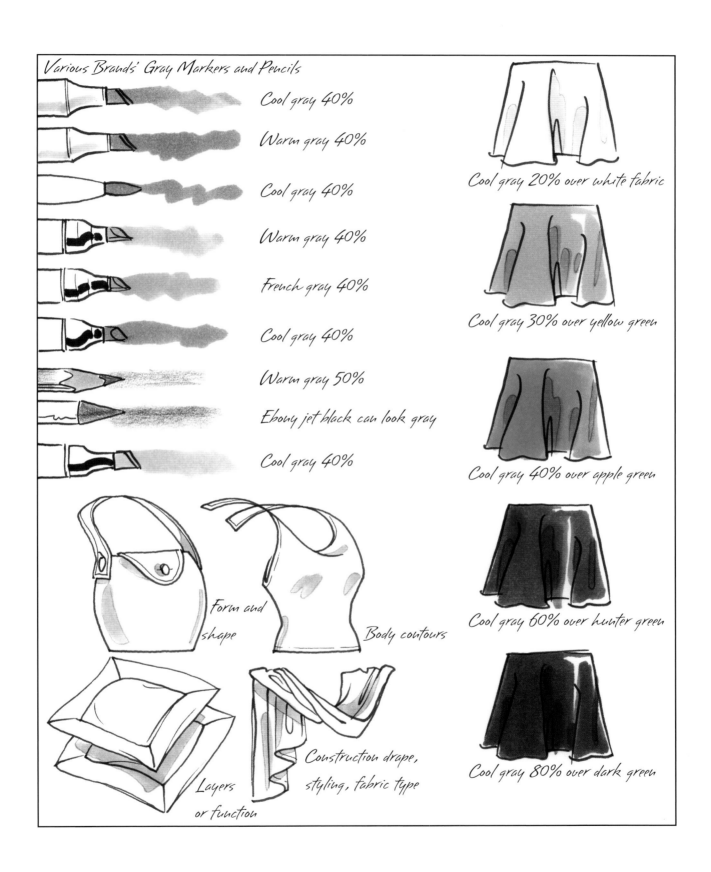

Various Brands' Gray Markers and Pencils

Cool gray 40%

Warm gray 40%

Cool gray 40%

Warm gray 40%

French gray 40%

Cool gray 40%

Warm gray 50%

Ebony jet black can look gray

Cool gray 40%

Form and shape

Body contours

Layers or function

Construction drape, styling, fabric type

Cool gray 20% over white fabric

Cool gray 30% over yellow green

Cool gray 40% over apple green

Cool gray 60% over hunter green

Cool gray 80% over dark green

Shading Methods

Shading can be independent of a specific light source direction. When you apply shading artfully, you can convey natural lighting. It's simply there, being used to emphasize construction, layering, or shape (form). The tailored examples below illustrate how shading can imply depth—in, out, over, and between layers of fabric.

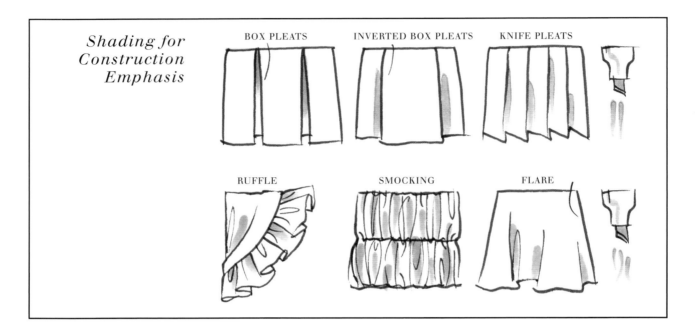

Shading can also go between layers as in the pillow example below. Add space or a top-to-bottom, above-and-below overlap. Notice how the shading bends around the chair example, rolling over the contours, demonstrating it has no sharp corners and focusing on how smooth its surface appears to be.

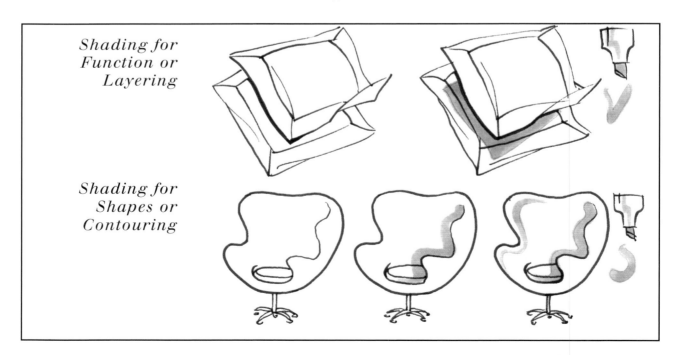

Practice shading unfinished, uncolored sketches. Work on creating some visual drama in strokes of gray that accentuate the crush in leather, or the drape in fabric. Gray strokes can also insinuate a light source which puts continuity in related shapes.

WARM GRAYS 30%

WEDGE TIPS

1. *Shading for Dramatic Effect*
2. *Shading for Fit and Drape*
3. *Shading for Light Source Continuity*

COOL GRAYS 30%

POINTED TIPS

Shading Options

Shading is often used as a stylistic preference. But done in conjunction with functional design, elements of shading can be informative. Style does add visual interest, but without emphasizing functional details, the power of your sketch can be diminished.

You can practice a variety of shading types, different accents for different reasons. There are a few examples on this page to work on. They show subtle changes in line or shape, and they are a valuable tool in building the storyline in design elements.

STYLE:
SOLID, FLAT COLOR
NO SHADING

FUNCTION:
VOLUME, THICKNESS
WITH SHADING
GRAY 40% ON FABRIC,
GRAY 70% ON WOOD TONE

GATHERS

SHIRRING

QUILTING

SHADING
BEHIND
FOLDS

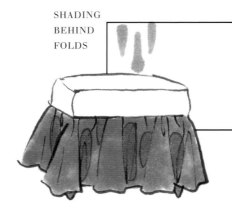

SHADING
INSIDE
GATHERS

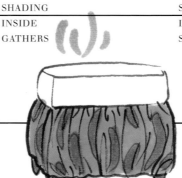

SHADING
INTO THE
STITCHES

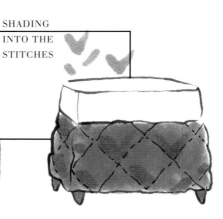

Shading for Drape

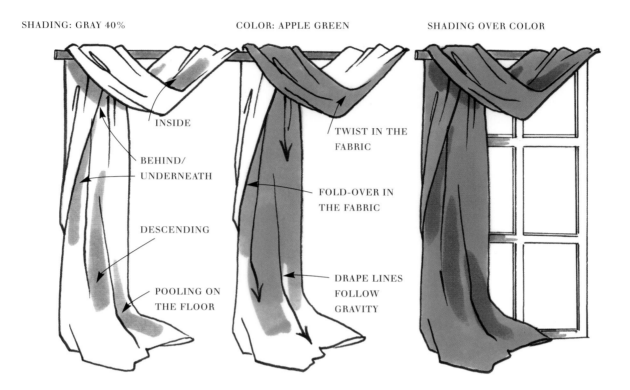

SHADING: GRAY 40%

INSIDE

BEHIND/
UNDERNEATH

DESCENDING

POOLING ON
THE FLOOR

COLOR: APPLE GREEN

TWIST IN THE
FABRIC

FOLD-OVER IN
THE FABRIC

DRAPE LINES
FOLLOW
GRAVITY

SHADING OVER COLOR

Shading can be done before or after you add color. After (or over color) is easier. Once you can see the value of your base layer in color, it is easier to calculate the number of the gray tone you should use to go over it. For example: 40 percent or lower for lighter colors and 50 percent or higher for deeper ones.

Shading has to convey major and minor differences in detail while alluding to dimensionality. These nuances in multiple shadows draw the focus from one point to another.

Shading for Layers: Creating Spaces between Things

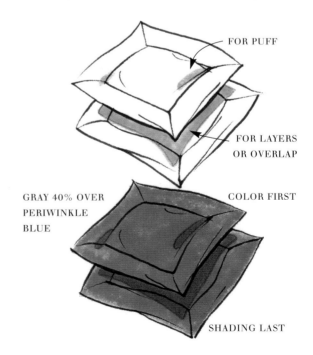

FOR PUFF

FOR LAYERS
OR OVERLAP

COLOR FIRST

GRAY 40% OVER
PERIWINKLE
BLUE

SHADING LAST

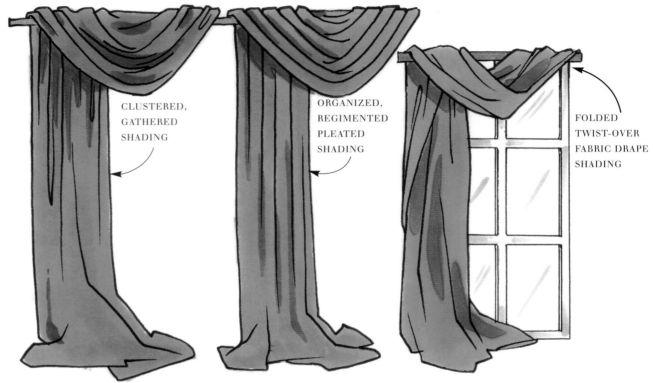

CLUSTERED, GATHERED SHADING

ORGANIZED, REGIMENTED PLEATED SHADING

FOLDED TWIST-OVER FABRIC DRAPE SHADING

Using Shadow to Create the Illusion of Drape without Construction

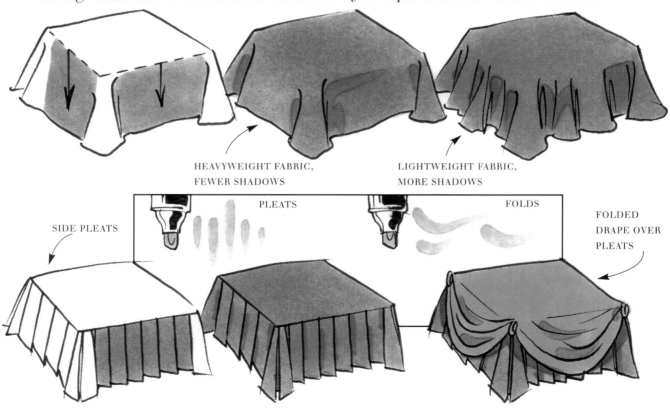

HEAVYWEIGHT FABRIC, FEWER SHADOWS

LIGHTWEIGHT FABRIC, MORE SHADOWS

SIDE PLEATS

PLEATS

FOLDS

FOLDED DRAPE OVER PLEATS

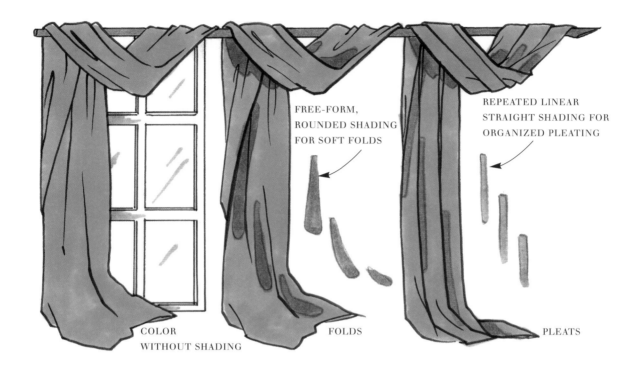

FREE-FORM,
ROUNDED SHADING
FOR SOFT FOLDS

REPEATED LINEAR
STRAIGHT SHADING FOR
ORGANIZED PLEATING

COLOR
WITHOUT SHADING

FOLDS

PLEATS

Shading Focus on Construction Detail

FOLD-OVER

FOLD-BACK

SHADING OVER
OR CLOSE TO THE
LINES OF DRAPE

SHADING TO
ACCENT FORM

POUF

SHADING
INTO BUNCHES
OF FABRIC

GATHERS

SHADING TO
FEATURE LAYERS
AND GATHERS

OVERLAP

A. Covered Chair

A. This chair has a design contrast between its stiff, straight top and its soft, gathered bottom. Shading here is done not just for style or light source but to illustrate these differences. Notice in the box at the right on this page that it takes three elements of line, color, and shading to convincingly display this drape.

B. This chair has no drape, but its smooth, molded contours need shading to convey how its armrest rolls into the curve of the seat cushion. Shading here adds dimension. Without it, the chair's surface would appear quite flat. It doesn't need as much shading as the chair above, but the shading is just as necessary to the chair's visual dynamics.

PEN LINE DRAPE

SHADING FOR DRAPE

SIZE FOR DRAPE

BASE COLOR

LOOSE COLOR OR PARTIAL RENDERING

B. Molded Chair

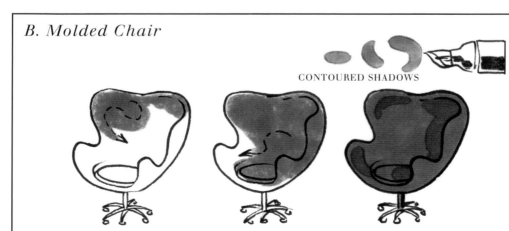

CONTOURED SHADOWS

Contoured Shading

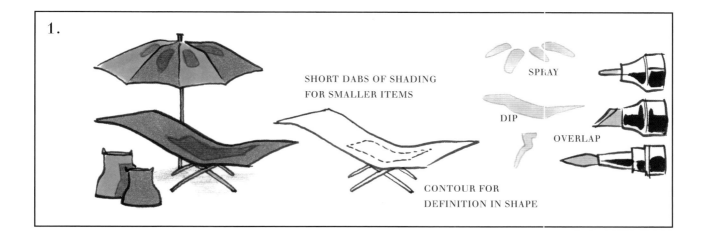

SHORT DABS OF SHADING
FOR SMALLER ITEMS

SPRAY

DIP

OVERLAP

CONTOUR FOR
DEFINITION IN SHAPE

1. Sometimes, as in a grouping of pieces, each item gets a different version of shading, a separate coloring technique. Here, for example, the umbrella gets a spray of shading for its sections. The chair gets a shadow to emphasize the dip in its seat. The pottery is shaded to explain the overlap.

2. Another creative use for shading is to explain unusual planes or angles. Shading here helps to define areas that defy classic perspective. Notice how the shading plumps up the back of the seat yet helps your eye roll across the arms of this chair.

LONG STROKES
FOR BIGGER ITEMS

CURVING
SHADOWS

CATCHING
LIGHT

PLANES

PLANES
WITHOUT
COLOR

COLOR
WITHOUT
PLANES

COMBINING
COLOR AND
PLANES

Shading for Accessories

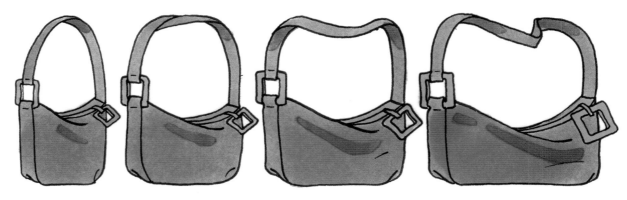

THE DEEPER THE FOLD, THE LONGER THE SHADOW

FOCUS ON THE
INNER POCKET

FOCUS ON THE
POUCHY GATHERS

FOCUS ON THE
POCKET FLAPS

Almost any design feature—the shape, cut, or volume—in accessories can benefit from the addition of shading to emphasize style, proportions, and materials. The examples on this page focus on the relationship between the shape or size of the particular handbag and its shading. The strap gets more shading as it gets larger. As the body of the bag gets bigger, it is given more shading to explain the soft fold in the middle of the shape. In the second row of handbags, the shading is used to accentuate design detail—to communicate style versus shape.

Practice Length and Variety in Your Shading Technique

Shading into the Bend

GRAY 60% ON APPLE GREEN/PERIWINKLE BLUE

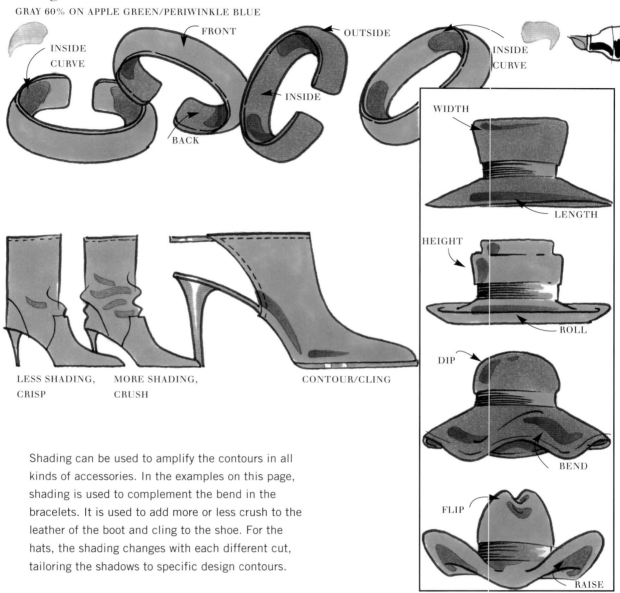

INSIDE CURVE

FRONT

OUTSIDE

INSIDE CURVE

INSIDE

BACK

WIDTH

LENGTH

HEIGHT

ROLL

DIP

BEND

FLIP

RAISE

LESS SHADING, CRISP

MORE SHADING, CRUSH

CONTOUR/CLING

SHADING USED HERE TO EMPHASIZE THE DESIGN FEATURES

Shading can be used to amplify the contours in all kinds of accessories. In the examples on this page, shading is used to complement the bend in the bracelets. It is used to add more or less crush to the leather of the boot and cling to the shoe. For the hats, the shading changes with each different cut, tailoring the shadows to specific design contours.

Single Strokes

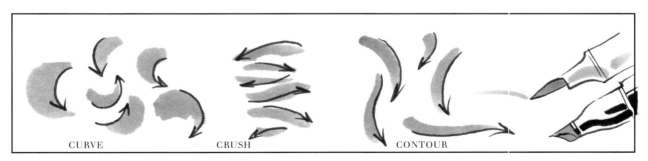

CURVE

CRUSH

CONTOUR

Shading for Fashion

So far you have learned to shade for construction, shape, and fabric weight. It's time to add figure shading to your list. Shading for body contours and clothes are the same. You shade to accent the curves in the body: the bustline or chest and the hip line. Then you use the bend in the elbow or the knee for drape or crush lines in the fabric. Shading for fashion is a mix of functional and decorative— functional to explain fit; decorative to keep the clothing from looking like cardboard cutouts.

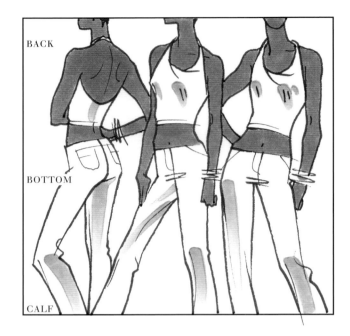

BACK

BOTTOM

CALF

FLESH TONES

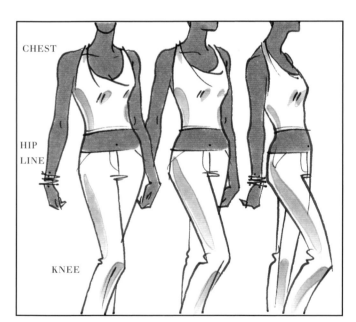

CHEST

HIP LINE

KNEE

Shading for Figure Contours
EXTRA FINE PEN POINT FOR ALL SEAM LINES

FUNCTIONAL   DECORATIVE

INTO THE
BUSTLINE DARTS

TO SOFTEN THE SILHOUETTE

PARTIAL RENDERING,
EMPHASIS ON FOLD

ACCENT ON WAISTLINE
FOR CLING AND FIT

Flats—Nonposed

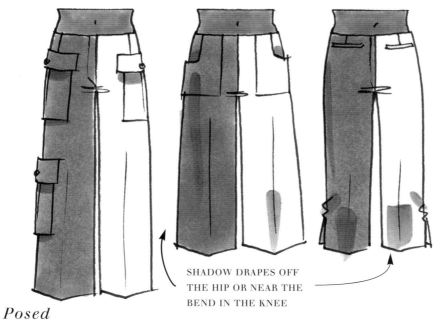

SHADING CAN BE SUBTLE AND DECORATIVE, ESPECIALLY ON FLATS. HERE YOU SHADE TO SUGGEST FABRIC FIT OR BEND TO KEEP FLATS FROM APPEARING STIFF.

SHADOW DRAPES OFF THE HIP OR NEAR THE BEND IN THE KNEE

Posed

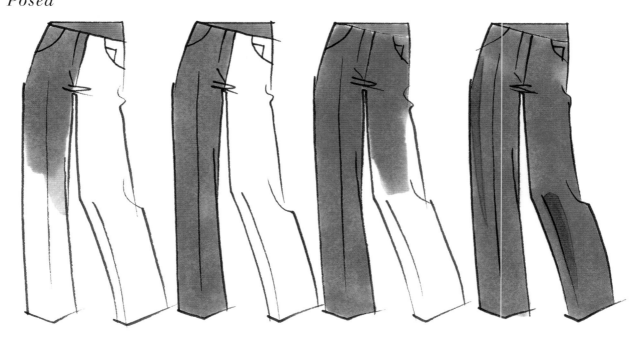

Practice Shading on Posed and Nonposed Shapes

REPEAT
LOOK-ALIKE
SHADOWS

FREE FORM SHADOWS

INTERIOR, INSIDE SHADOWS

LINEAR, STRUCTURED SHADOWS

ASCENDING SHADING
FOLLOWS THE DRAPE
INTO THE KNOT

DESCENDING SHADING

CLUSTERED SHADING AT THE WAISTLINE GATHERS
PLUS DESCENDING SHADOWS FOR THE FOLDS

DIRECTIONAL SHADING

HEAVY TO LIGHT

CLUSTERED

DESCENDING

LIGHT TO HEAVY

DIRECTIONAL

SHADE BELOW AND
UNDERNEATH THE TUCKS

MULTIPLE SHADOWS
FOR CRYSTAL PLEATS

SHADE INSIDE, IN BETWEEN
THE BOX PLEAT PANELS

DESCENDING SHADING IN THE DIRECTION
OF THE SIDE PLEATS THAT MOVE TO THE RIGHT

SARONG—SHADE INTO
THE DRAPE LINES

ASYMMETRICAL—
SHADE BEHIND THE FOLDS

GATHERS—SHADE INTO THE WAISTLINE
DOWN TOWARD THE HEMLINE

FLARE—START SHADING FROM THE HIGH HIP SIDE

PRACTICE VARIETY

Complex Shading

There are instances in which you will be using shading as part of a layered or complex rendering technique. In the examples shown here, solid coloring has been altered to reflect light or to demonstrate degrees of transparency versus solid, opaque materials. With materials like plastics in Lucite or vinyls, or gauzy fabrics like chiffons, shading becomes a critical part of the rendering process—the last step (or second to last step when you're using a colored pencil) that brings the sketch to life. The shadows on these things are subtle but integral to creating the illusion of transparency. (More on that in Chapter 7.)

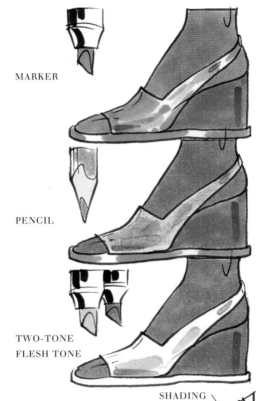

MARKER

PENCIL

TWO-TONE
FLESH TONE

SHADING
GRAY 60%

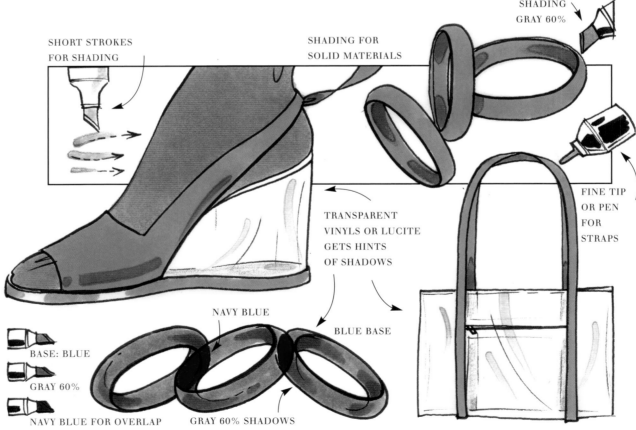

SHORT STROKES
FOR SHADING

SHADING FOR
SOLID MATERIALS

TRANSPARENT
VINYLS OR LUCITE
GETS HINTS
OF SHADOWS

FINE TIP
OR PEN
FOR
STRAPS

NAVY BLUE

BLUE BASE

BASE: BLUE

GRAY 60%

NAVY BLUE FOR OVERLAP

GRAY 60% SHADOWS

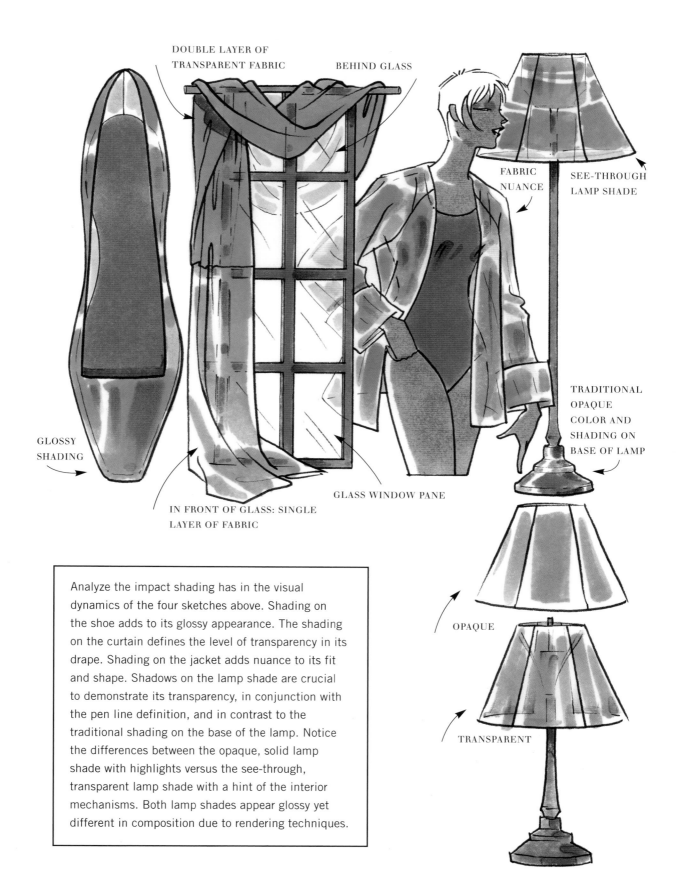

DOUBLE LAYER OF
TRANSPARENT FABRIC

BEHIND GLASS

FABRIC
NUANCE

SEE-THROUGH
LAMP SHADE

GLOSSY
SHADING

GLASS WINDOW PANE

IN FRONT OF GLASS: SINGLE
LAYER OF FABRIC

TRADITIONAL
OPAQUE
COLOR AND
SHADING ON
BASE OF LAMP

OPAQUE

TRANSPARENT

Analyze the impact shading has in the visual dynamics of the four sketches above. Shading on the shoe adds to its glossy appearance. The shading on the curtain defines the level of transparency in its drape. Shading on the jacket adds nuance to its fit and shape. Shadows on the lamp shade are crucial to demonstrate its transparency, in conjunction with the pen line definition, and in contrast to the traditional shading on the base of the lamp. Notice the differences between the opaque, solid lamp shade with highlights versus the see-through, transparent lamp shade with a hint of the interior mechanisms. Both lamp shades appear glossy yet different in composition due to rendering techniques.

Assignment

Practice basic shading placement in conjunction with fabric and construction. Notice that in each example, as you modify the shading to the drape, the tailoring, or the volume, you amplify the design detail. That is the point of doing shading. The only pitfall is doing too much of it so that the fabric looks wrinkled or too little so that the fabric looks wooden.

First, practice loose, short strokes of gray. Second, work out three rows of fabric in simple forms with a variety of construction types. Third, practice adding shadows to these forms in various degrees of rendered states. Leave some blank so that you can really see the shading and get used to its flow across the color—some in partial or full color to analyze how shading works best on them. For drape without construction or just planes or sides, color only the angle of drape so that you see how the shading helps to visually describe folds.

CHAPTER 4

LAYERED

COLOR

Checklist for Layering Colors

Markers When working on complicated multitoned illustrations, gather your supplies in one area on your desk so that everything you need is in one place. This will save you time and aggravation by always having *what* you need *when* you need it

As you color test your supplies for a specific illustration, list and label every color so that you can remember what you want to use and what you don't. Consider this work page or your notes as a vital piece of paper for the task at hand.

You have to test color on top of color to see which colors blend, disappear, or have just the right amount of contrast. Again, you have to label these by marker brand and color name or number. Next you have to remember to note the order in which you are going to use these colors—first, middle, and last.

It's also good to note on your test sheet what type of nib or brush tip gave you the surface interest you were looking for, including in its specific color.

Remember to clean off the (smudged) tips of the lighter colored markers whenever they are used too close to dark colors or pencil. Just rub the tip back and forth over a tissue or clean piece of scrap paper until it looks clear of smudges.

Pencils Be careful not to drop colored pencils. Their leads can be fragile and crack inside their wood casings. This leads to lots of frustration when you sharpen them and they keep breaking.

Keep a sharpener handy as you are working. The larger the area you have to cover or the more times you use your colored pencils, the duller those soft leads will get. Hand-held sharpeners are the best because you can control the process with gentle pressure and care.

Blow or wipe a colored pencil's tip off after sharpening it. This takes away any loose lead that could possibly smear on your page as you work.

Paper Not all brands of marker paper are interchangeable. This can present a problem if you try to use papers from two different companies in one presentation. Each brand of marker paper has a different degree of whiteness and absorbs or reflects color differently. For example, blue marker, or even pencil, could look darker on one brand of paper than on another.

Test Page

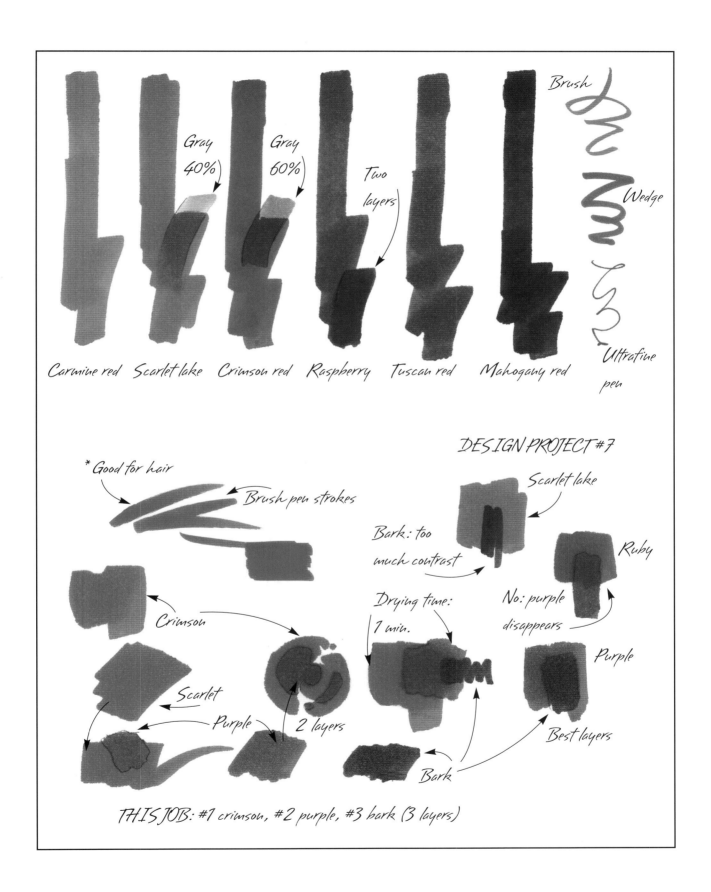

Gray 40%)

Gray 60%)

Two layers

Carmine red   Scarlet lake   Crimson red   Raspberry   Tuscan red   Mahogany red

Brush

Wedge

Ultrafine pen

DESIGN PROJECT #7

* Good for hair

Brush pen strokes

Scarlet lake

Bark: too much contrast

Ruby

Crimson

Drying time: 1 min.

No: purple disappears

Purple

Scarlet

Purple

2 layers

Best layers

Bark

THIS JOB: #1 crimson, #2 purple, #3 bark (3 layers)

Layered Color — Three-Step Reds

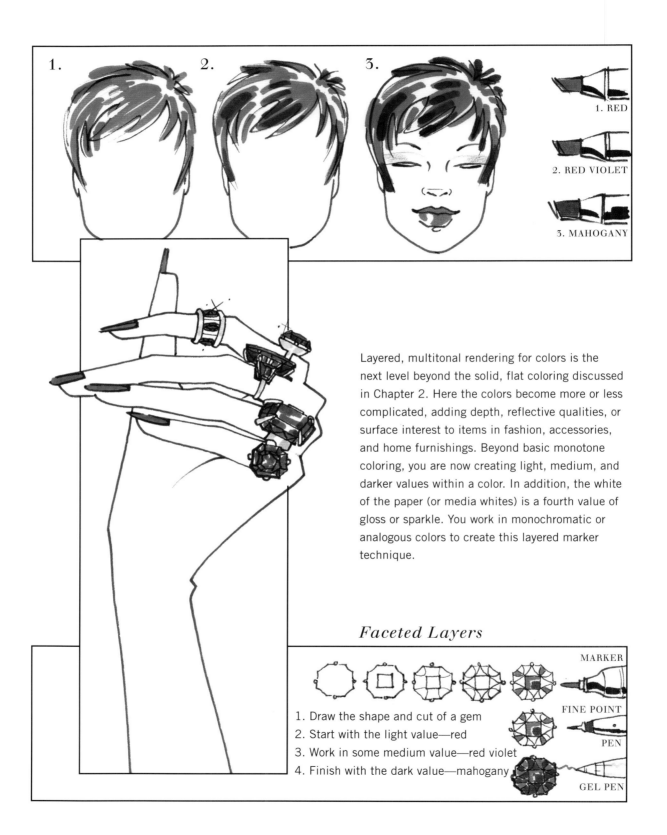

1.
2.
3.

1. RED

2. RED VIOLET

3. MAHOGANY

Layered, multitonal rendering for colors is the next level beyond the solid, flat coloring discussed in Chapter 2. Here the colors become more or less complicated, adding depth, reflective qualities, or surface interest to items in fashion, accessories, and home furnishings. Beyond basic monotone coloring, you are now creating light, medium, and darker values within a color. In addition, the white of the paper (or media whites) is a fourth value of gloss or sparkle. You work in monochromatic or analogous colors to create this layered marker technique.

Faceted Layers

MARKER

FINE POINT

PEN

GEL PEN

1. Draw the shape and cut of a gem
2. Start with the light value—red
3. Work in some medium value—red violet
4. Finish with the dark value—mahogany

Reds

SMOOTH   FACETED   DIRECTIONAL   CONTOURED

Gemstones

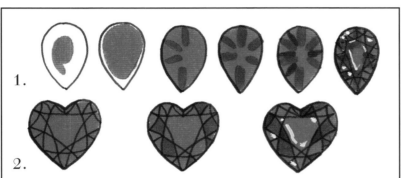

CRIMSON

PURPLE

MAHOGANY

1. **Three layers, Loose technique:** Solid color base working from the inside out. Angular, spears of colors in alternating positions. Use line for facet details. Add white gel pen for sparkle.

2. **Three layers, tight technique:** Solid color base over black line facet details. Drop second and third value colors into alternating cuts. Use white gel pen for sparkle.

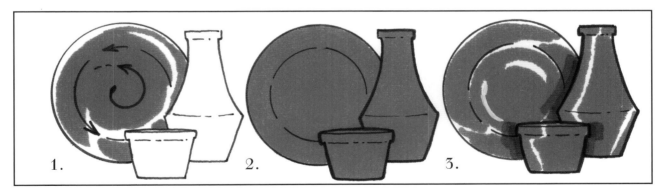

1. **One layer, glossy:** Color from the inside out in a circular motion leaving contoured highlights that mimic the shape.

2. **One layer, flat:** Color edge to edge with just the base color. No highlights or shading.

3. **Two layers (plus highlights):** Color in a circular motion or imitate the contours of the item for highlighting. Use shadow to separate the pieces from each other and to suggest space.

Shading Options — Browns

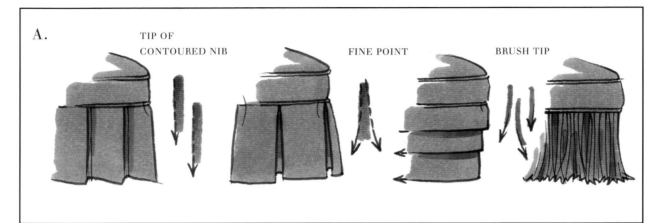

A.

TIP OF CONTOURED NIB   FINE POINT   BRUSH TIP

B.

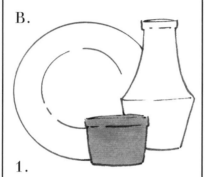

1.

2.

3.

This page and the page opposite focus on the intent or content of shading. The shading may be functional for detail emphasis or decorative for style. It may also enhance the quality of a color. Regardless of the purpose, shading will make it possible for you to maximize the visual interest in a specific color.

On this page examples A and C illustrate functional shading for construction details. Example B uses functional shading to visually explain space between objects. The illustrations on page 81 use shading to enhance the surface qualities in a variety of looks for a specific color.

Shading for Depth of Field or Space

1. **Foreground:** The cup nearest or closest to view gets the lightest value.
2. **Middleground:** The carafe is in between the plate and cup. It gets the middle value.
3. **Background:** The plate is the farthest back from view so it gets the darkest value.

C.

SMOOTH SHINY DIRECTIONAL CONTOURED

Options for Rendering Hair

LIGHT TAN

BARK

DARK BROWN

Three values:
Light, middle, and
dark to give brown
hair its highlights or
glossy look.

ONE LAYER
Loose, partial
rendering using
white of page as
shine on hair.

TWO LAYERS
Accent on the
middle of head
provides more
shape in the
hairstyle.

THREE LAYERS
Finished, tight
rendering that
darkens the tips
of hair to frame
the face.

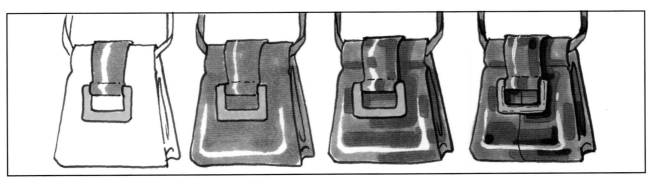

 LINE VARIETY WITH THICKER
POINT: OUTLINE OUTER EDGE

 EXTRA-FINE POINT:
INTERIOR LINES

Layered Rendering for Black and Gray

You can use an alternative method for layered, value-based, rendering for deep, dark colors, especially black, grays, and navies (see Chapter 6). For this reverse coloring process, you start with the darkest value instead of the lightest. This way you can estimate how to use as much of the darkest value while still being able to see details. Examples A, B, and C illustrate some of the options in layering color. Example D shows you the monochromatic light to dark layering technique for dark, glossy fabrics. As you progress from the light color to the dark color, you will add to the reflective quality of the fabric by using highlights and shadows.

Options

A. B. C.

ADD DRYING TIME
BETWEEN APPLICATION
OF EACH MARKER LAYER

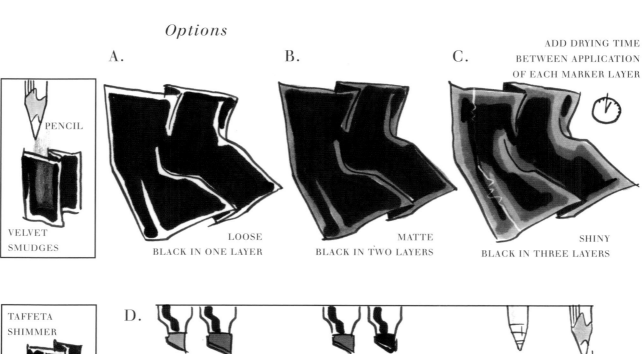

PENCIL

VELVET
SMUDGES

LOOSE
BLACK IN ONE LAYER

MATTE
BLACK IN TWO LAYERS

SHINY
BLACK IN THREE LAYERS

D.

TAFFETA
SHIMMER

GEL
PEN

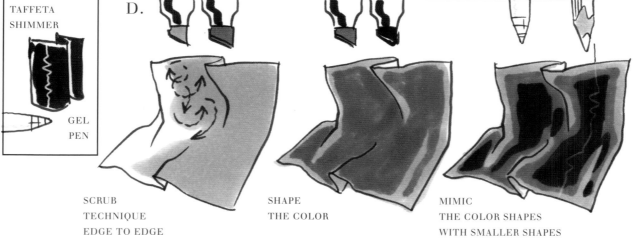

SCRUB
TECHNIQUE
EDGE TO EDGE

SHAPE
THE COLOR

MIMIC
THE COLOR SHAPES
WITH SMALLER SHAPES

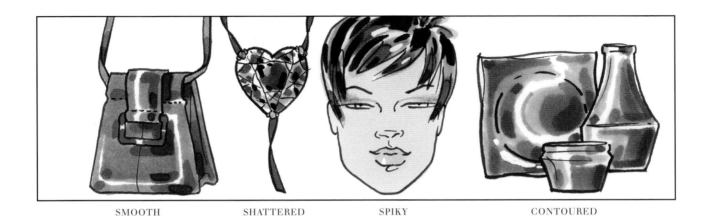

SMOOTH   SHATTERED   SPIKY   CONTOURED

Using Gray as a Background Color for Black

GRAY 40%

GRAY 60%

BLACK

BRUSH PEN

There are all types of grays in a variety of values. Almost any gray in two or three values can achieve the same results for any of the examples on this page.

A.   B.   C.

The hair rendering in A was done in two steps; example B, in one step. Both get the same results, which proves that in example C you get a beautiful look using either method.

GRAY 40%   GRAY 60%   BLACK BRUSH PEN
SILKY BLACK

Reflective or Glossy Yellows

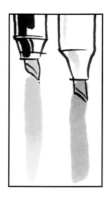

Multitonal rendering is all about choice. You select the number of values or layers you want to use to enhance the coloring in any design category. It will run the gamut from too little to just right to overworked. Between a loose or tight finish you are going to have to strike a balance in your work to fit your style.

Notice on this page that adding highlights or the use of the white of the page appears as a fourth value. You commit to this look during the rendering of the lightest value, or you do it last using a white gel pen over the marker colors. The first row illustrates how to use layered coloring to imitate the light-catching quality of some fabrics. The second row shows the extra step in rendering weave or print detail.

Introducing a Fourth Value — Highlighting

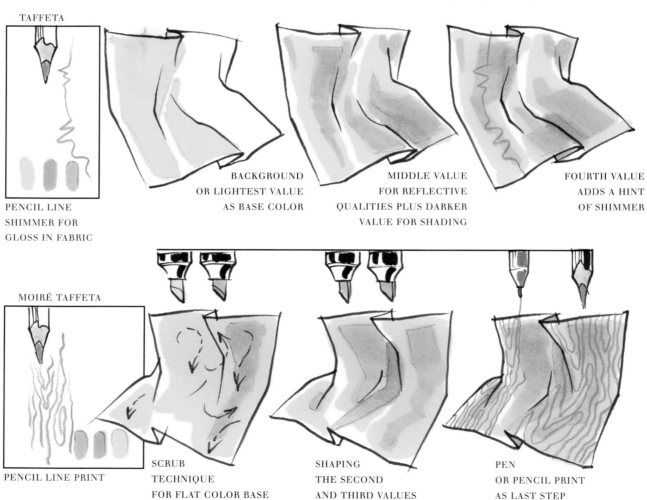

TAFFETA

PENCIL LINE
SHIMMER FOR
GLOSS IN FABRIC

BACKGROUND
OR LIGHTEST VALUE
AS BASE COLOR

MIDDLE VALUE
FOR REFLECTIVE
QUALITIES PLUS DARKER
VALUE FOR SHADING

FOURTH VALUE
ADDS A HINT
OF SHIMMER

MOIRÉ TAFFETA

PENCIL LINE PRINT

SCRUB
TECHNIQUE
FOR FLAT COLOR BASE

SHAPING
THE SECOND
AND THIRD VALUES

PEN
OR PENCIL PRINT
AS LAST STEP

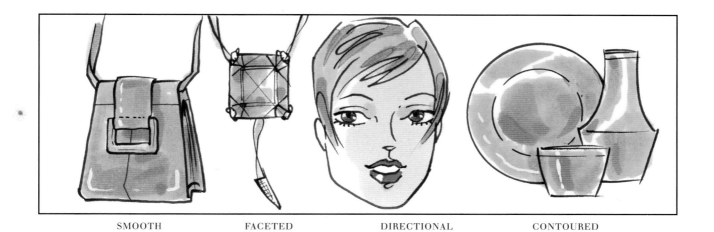

| SMOOTH | FACETED | DIRECTIONAL | CONTOURED |

Color Test

LABEL YOUR CHOICES WITH MARKER NAME, NUMBER, AND SEQUENCE OF USE

| LEMON YELLOW | SPANISH ORANGE | PALE SEPIA | CADMIUM ORANGE |

| START | ONE LAYER | TWO LAYERS | THREE LAYERS |

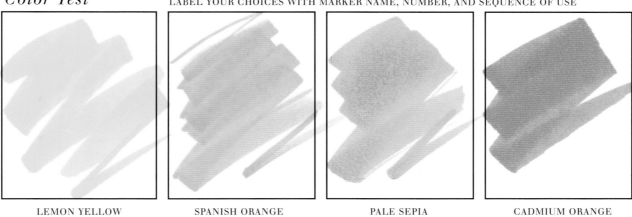

The lists of monochromatic or analogous looking colors in this chapter are only suggestions. You can always make up your own values or color versions of this range in layered, multitonal rendering, especially if you are trying to match a specific color from a swatch or sample for a design project.

Special Effects over Layered Color

FABRIC SWATCH

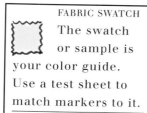

The swatch or sample is your color guide. Use a test sheet to match markers to it.

TIME BETWEEN LAYERS

Best to leave at least a minute for marker (or three minutes for pen) to dry between layers.

LIGHT SOURCE

Use the same light source in a grouping. Use the side opposite the light for shading.

BASE:
LEMON YELLOW

ACCENT: SPANISH
ORANGE

SHADING:
PALE SEPIA

LARGE DOTS

SMALL DOTS

SEQUINS
IN PEN OR PENCIL

To create a look that includes the surface interest of luxe fabrics like velvets, faille, jacquards, and sequins, you add the appearance of luminosity or iridescence to your coloring. This rendering process can be in three steps for print or texture plus background color. Of course, you can take shortcuts in these techniques to fit time, style, or portfolio considerations.

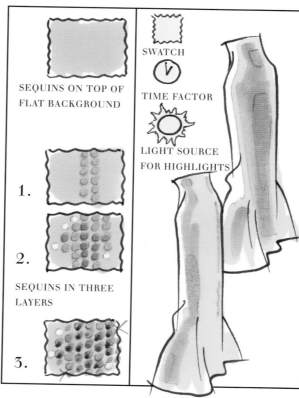

SEQUINS ON TOP OF
FLAT BACKGROUND

1.

2.

SEQUINS IN THREE
LAYERS

3.

SWATCH

TIME FACTOR

LIGHT SOURCE
FOR HIGHLIGHTS

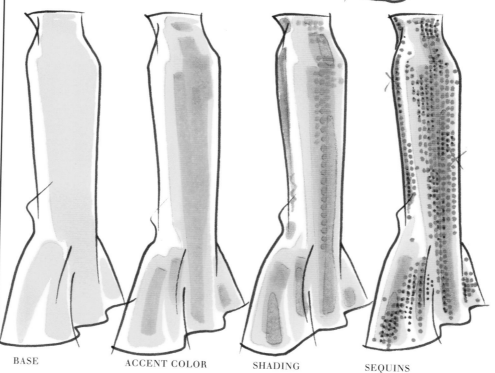

BASE   ACCENT COLOR   SHADING   SEQUINS

Solid Color
Backgrounds

Tonal Backgrounds

FAILLE

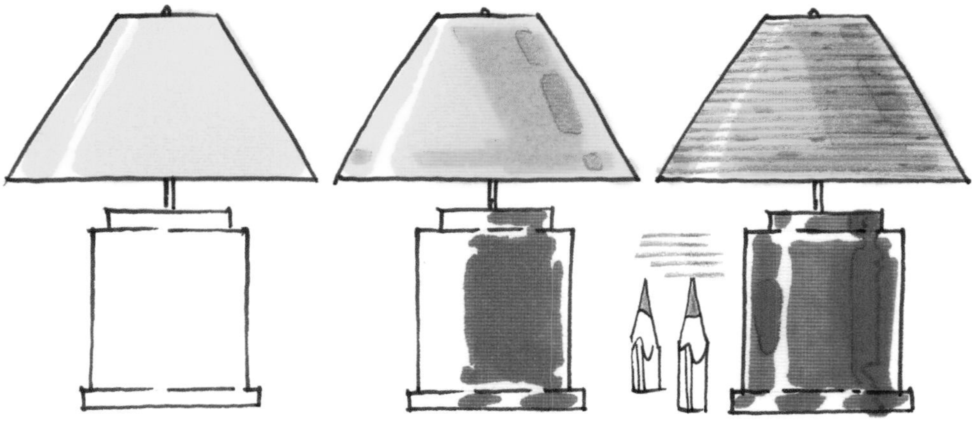

JACQUARD PRINT

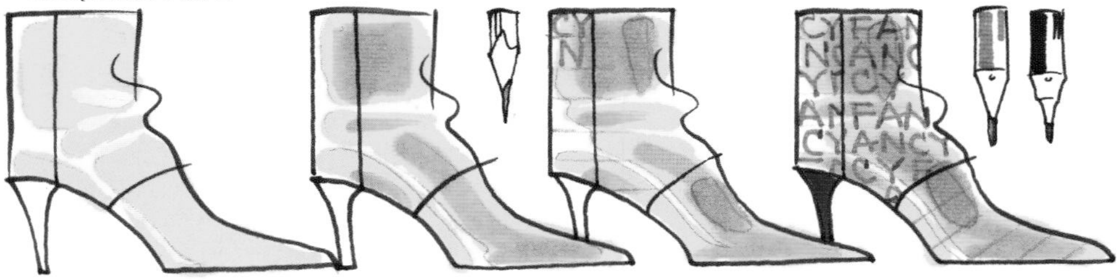

CRUSHED VELVET

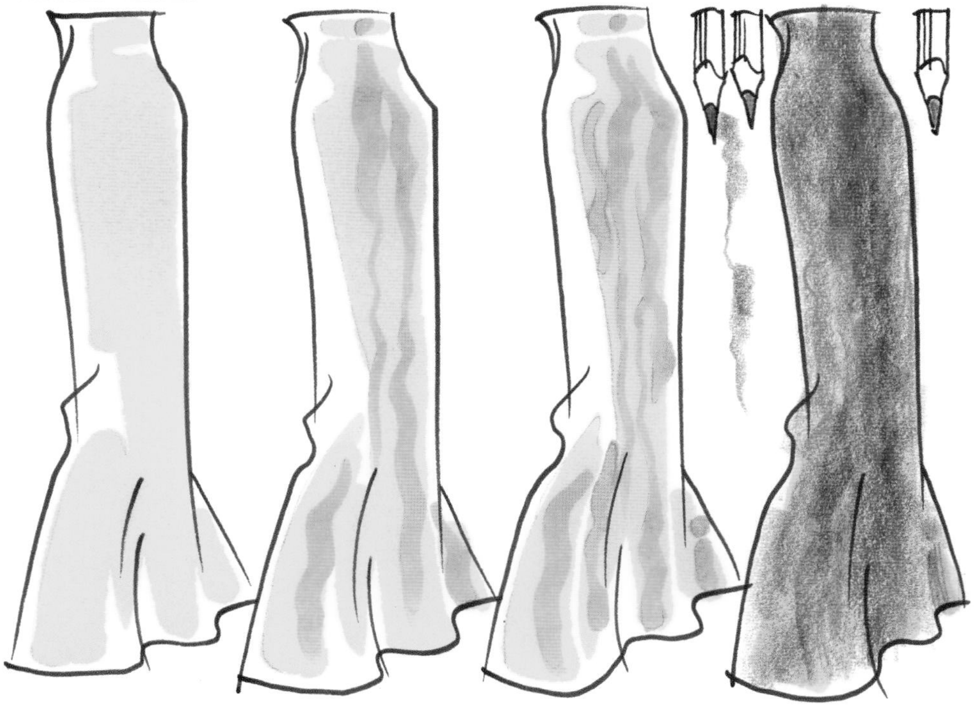

Rendering Overlays

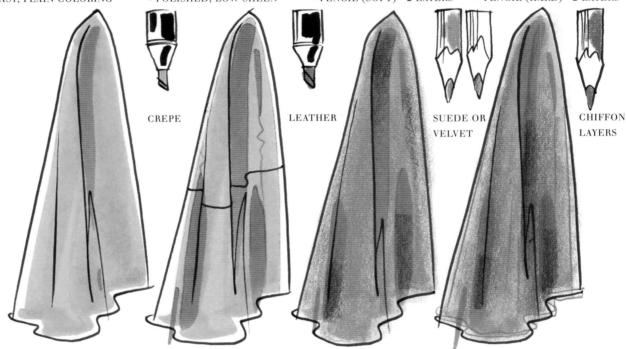

CASUAL FABRIC:
- MARKER—2 LAYERS
- EASY, PLAIN COLORING

LEATHER:
- MARKER—2 LAYERS
- POLISHED, LOW SHEEN

CREPE

GRAINY TEXTURE:
- MARKER—2 LAYERS
- PENCIL (SOFT)—2 LAYERS

LEATHER

CHIFFON LAYERS:
- MARKER—2 LAYERS
- PENCIL (HARD)—2 LAYERS

SUEDE OR
VELVET

CHIFFON
LAYERS

Matte Colors
- No need to reflect light.
- Gets smooth, flat coloring.
- Conservative shading in gray or analogous colors.

Low Sheen
- Contrast between color and shadows generous, to establish depth to color.
- Use related colors to enhance coloring.
- This is the method to establish the base coloring for more complex rendering treatments.

Brushed Surfaces
- First, simple layer is pencil over marker.
- Need two pencil colors for base and shadow colors that have to ride over the marker coloring.
- Here's where pens and pencils can be used to create myriad surface treatments.

Grainy Texture
- Vastly different materials get similar rendering tricks.
- Use side of pencil lead to create the look of nap, weave, or brushed surfaces.
- Use pencil point to draw extra hemlines or overlays for chiffon layers over another fabric.

RIBBON CHIFFON
OVERLAY (BRUSHED
SURFACE BASE):
- BASE (MARKER)—
  2 LAYERS
- OVERLAY (PENCIL)—
  2 METHODS

LACE OVER JACQUARD
PRINT (LOW SHEEN BASE):
- BASE (MARKER)—
  2 LAYERS
- BASE PRINT (PEN)—
  2 LAYERS

LACE OVER SILK CHARMEUSE
(MATTE COLOR BASE):
- BASE (MARKER)—2 LAYERS
- LACE INTERIOR (PENCIL)—
  CROSS HATCH
- LACE REPEATS—PEN LINE

CUT VELVET OVER SILK
(GRAINY TEXTURE BASE):
- BASE (MARKER)—2 LAYERS
- VELVET BACKGROUND—
  PENCIL
- VELVET PRINT—PENCIL LINE
- BEADING—WHITE GEL PEN

Ribbon Effect　　*Transparent Lace*　　*Lace Trim*　　*Cut Dévoré Velvet*

Pens

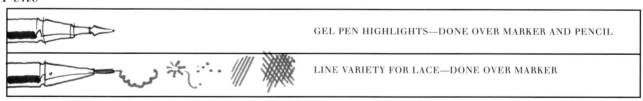

GEL PEN HIGHLIGHTS—DONE OVER MARKER AND PENCIL

LINE VARIETY FOR LACE—DONE OVER MARKER

Pencils

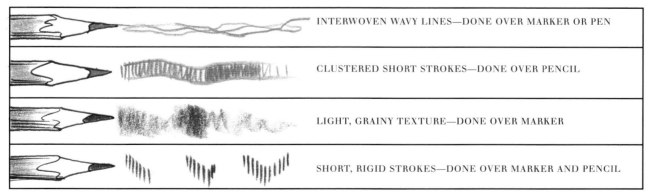

INTERWOVEN WAVY LINES—DONE OVER MARKER OR PEN

CLUSTERED SHORT STROKES—DONE OVER PENCIL

LIGHT, GRAINY TEXTURE—DONE OVER MARKER

SHORT, RIGID STROKES—DONE OVER MARKER AND PENCIL

Prints in Layered Rendering

Jacquards/Damasks/Brocades

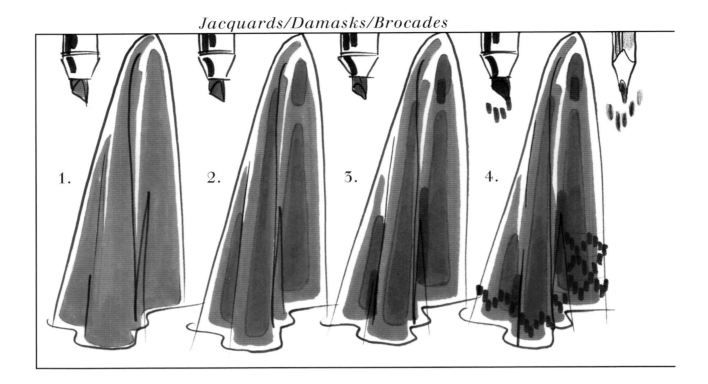

Dobby Weave

Color on Color—
Quick Rendering

One of the most challenging fabrics is a dobby weave with same color contrast that can be seen only when the fabric catches light. The marker solution is to use three tones of the same color, as shown here, to illustrate this print.

1. Base or background color, leaving light where the print will show up in step 3.
2. Drop in some deep shadows.
3. & 4. Map in the print. There are only three steps here. Step 3 was just to slow down the process for better instructive value.

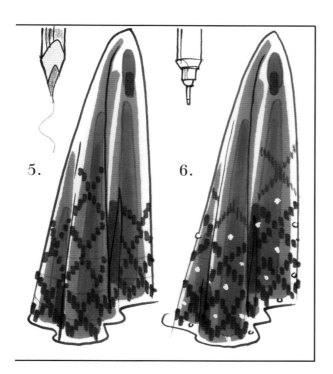

Raised Prints or Weaves

To keep rendering looking fresh and loose versus tight or overworked under all this technique, leave lots of highlights in the base color layer. Don't color too near the outline edge but let the interior get enough shadow.

1. Let the base color catch light.
2. Mimic the base color's shape in small increments.
3. Push the shadows up against folds.
4. In 4H pencil, plan how the print is going to be affected by any drape.
5. Finish the print.
6. Add extra details with gel pen.

Open Weaves

Rendering lace combines fine-line cross-hatching with print repeats. It may also include delicate scalloped edging. Any background or base color done in marker will have to go on first because most pens will run under marker coloring.

1. Establish the repeat print in the scalloped edging in pencil.
2. Draw the detailing for the repeat print.
3. Carefully fill in the cross-hatching without losing the print details.

Lace

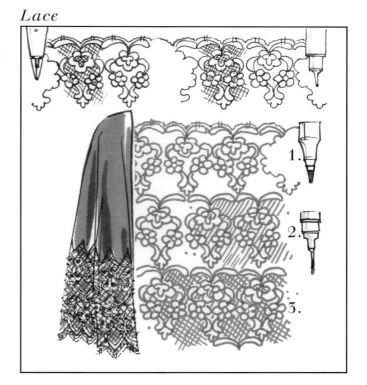

Shading

Lots of items need shading to complete the expression of dimension in the sketch. This spread adds to what you practiced in Chapter 3.

A. Body Contour

With lots of print layers to render, you can stop in the middle, to drop in shading. If you do it quickly using few strokes, you will not smear the base coat color.

Use a stronger color for your body contour shading than you use for the solid color base. This shadow may look overpowering at first but it has to stand up to the print that will be rendered over it. After you finish filling in the print, the shadow will melt into the background.

B. Accessory Shaping

Try using the shading first to deepen the inside curve so that the outside curve pops. Use another shadow underneath a bead to make it look more three dimensional. Once you finish the exterior coloring and the interior shading, make the outlines bolder where there are surface or color changes.

C. Iridescent Coloring

Some fabrics or materials have a two-tone color that almost defies rendering. You need to randomly spread the two tones across your silhouette, blending them as you finish coloring in the shape. Although the coloring looks different, the shading technique won't. You still move under or between design layers.

Remember to test the two colors together on a test sheet before beginning your sketch. When you begin rendering, work with the lighter of the two colors first so that marker tip isn't ruined by the darker color. Leave lots of empty spaces to blend in the second, darker color. Shading is the third, and last, layer.

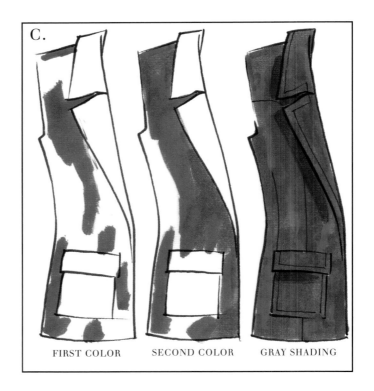

FIRST COLOR   SECOND COLOR   GRAY SHADING

1. Beads

In a limited space, coloring can be tight work. In the contrast between a raised and flat surface, in a small area, you can use shading to make something pop from the background's flat surface.

2. Buttons

Like beads, buttons have enough volume and design focus to merit the attention of dimensional shading.

3. Levels or Layers

When you have a lot of dimensional detail in a small or tight space, you need to emphasize those design features with a specific type of shading. This applies to overlap, overhang, or other decorative elements between layers.

Materials may change within the design premise, but in illustration the shading technique remains the same for all features in your sketch.

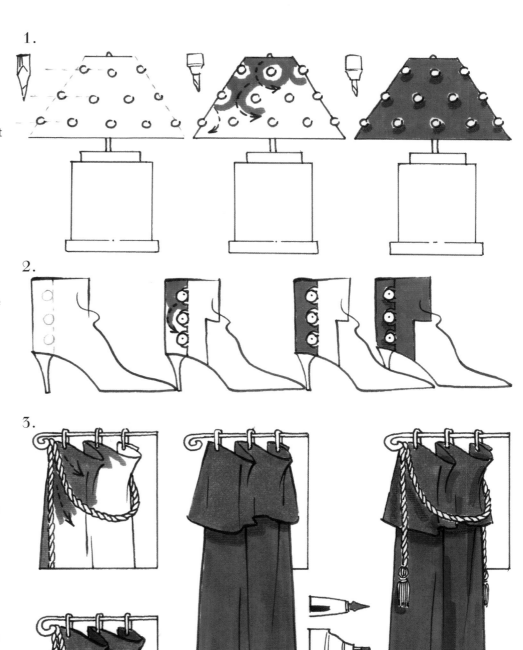

Mixing Marker, Pencil, and Pen

There are a number of rendering challenges that include pencil, pen, and brush pen techniques to complete the look you want to create. Pattern and texture variety are created by mixing your media and layering your colors.

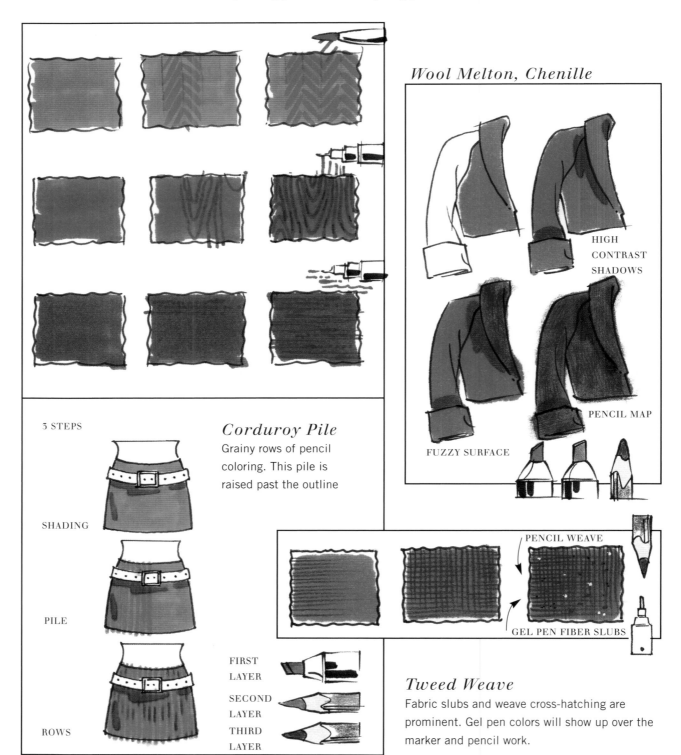

Wool Melton, Chenille

HIGH CONTRAST SHADOWS

PENCIL MAP

FUZZY SURFACE

Corduroy Pile

Grainy rows of pencil coloring. This pile is raised past the outline

3 STEPS

SHADING

PILE

ROWS

FIRST LAYER

SECOND LAYER

THIRD LAYER

PENCIL WEAVE

GEL PEN FIBER SLUBS

Tweed Weave

Fabric slubs and weave cross-hatching are prominent. Gel pen colors will show up over the marker and pencil work.

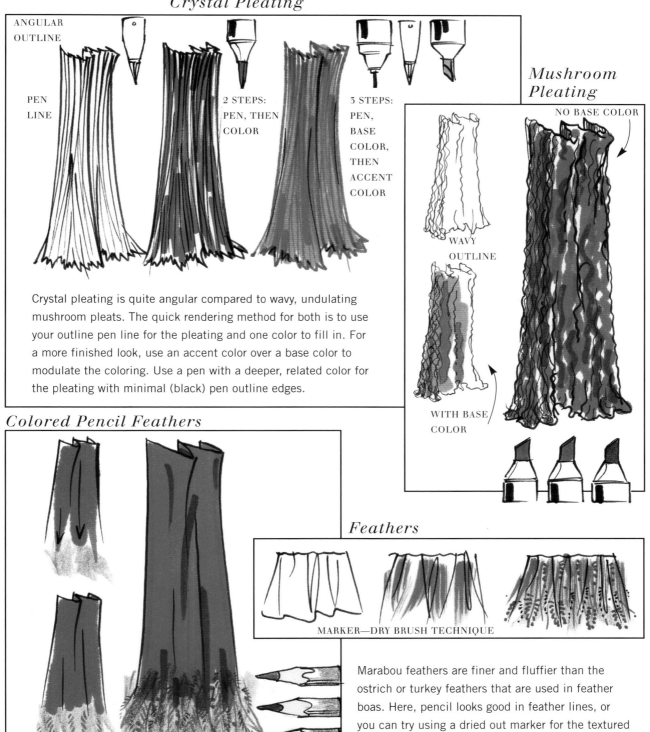

Crystal Pleating

ANGULAR
OUTLINE

PEN
LINE

2 STEPS:
PEN, THEN
COLOR

3 STEPS:
PEN,
BASE
COLOR,
THEN
ACCENT
COLOR

Crystal pleating is quite angular compared to wavy, undulating mushroom pleats. The quick rendering method for both is to use your outline pen line for the pleating and one color to fill in. For a more finished look, use an accent color over a base color to modulate the coloring. Use a pen with a deeper, related color for the pleating with minimal (black) pen outline edges.

Mushroom Pleating

NO BASE COLOR

WAVY
OUTLINE

WITH BASE
COLOR

Colored Pencil Feathers

Feathers

MARKER—DRY BRUSH TECHNIQUE

Marabou feathers are finer and fluffier than the ostrich or turkey feathers that are used in feather boas. Here, pencil looks good in feather lines, or you can try using a dried out marker for the textured coloring that feathers need.

Rendering Skills and Artistry

With the instructions in Chapters 1–4 you have, by now, a full range of applications for solid color rendering. Looking from left to right over this spread, you can see this range, from a simple solid red to the glamour production red. It's all about options from working in one layer to four layers or matte to glossy. Notice another option—the matte red is rendered tightly, edge to edge. The glossy red is rendered loosely, with some white visible throughout the shapes.

Scrub Technique
Work your way down into the hemline

Matte Red
Smooth, solid, flat color for a fabric like crepe

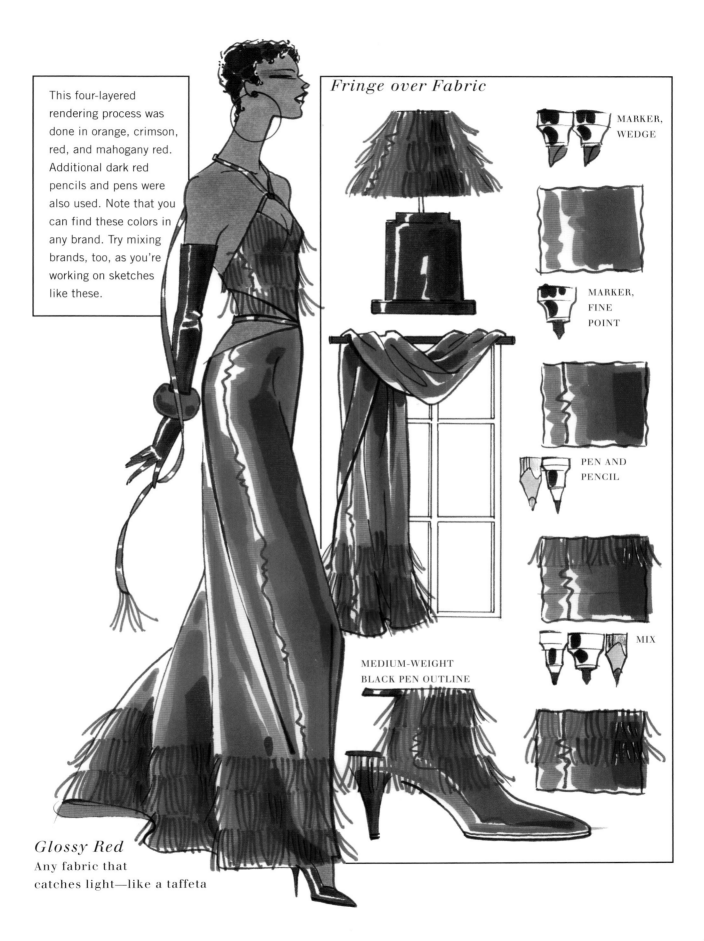

This four-layered rendering process was done in orange, crimson, red, and mahogany red. Additional dark red pencils and pens were also used. Note that you can find these colors in any brand. Try mixing brands, too, as you're working on sketches like these.

Fringe over Fabric

MARKER, WEDGE

MARKER, FINE POINT

PEN AND PENCIL

MIX

MEDIUM-WEIGHT BLACK PEN OUTLINE

Glossy Red
Any fabric that catches light—like a taffeta

Assignment

Crossover in most design fields continues to grow. This is a result of merging lifestyles and products through the cachet of logo, taste, and attitude. This means that you never know what you'll be asked to design from a style perspective. To prepare you for the crossover, for this assignment, you should make one swatch do it all in the design divisions of fashion, accessories, and home fashions.

Find a swatch of material that challenges your sense of color and rendering skills. Then do the following:

- Map out three or four rendering steps.
- Label the marker color names, brands, and tips. Also list your pencils and pens, if you need them to complete this sample.
- Design three simple shapes, one for each design category.
- Render the three designs.

Regardless of your sketching abilities, your color rendering should have equal visual power for all three designs.

STRIPES
AND
PRINTS

CHAPTER 5

Checklist for Stripes and Prints

Pens   Try not to take your pen for granted. A company could change its ink, pen point, or color between the time you finish using an old pen and buy a new one. Also new pens can sometimes be oddly too dry or too wet. Too wet causes the ink to spray a bit when you apply pressure on your line. This is to remind you that you should always test check new pens. Trial and error are fine as long as it's not on your best work.

Pen points have features that are often best suited to specific tasks. Also, since some are not bleed-proof (will run under marker), you have to remember to use them only after you have completed all your marker coloring in the area in which you are about to use that kind of pen line.

Don't leave the cap off a drawing (versus writing) pen for too long—too long is a few hours. Pens can be vulnerable to drying out, the black ink goes a bit gray, or the point clogs. If you apply too much pressure as you draw, the pen's point can fray or retreat back into its (metal) casing. This is one of the reasons it's always appropriate to have duplicates of your favorite pens (buy them by the box).

Keep in mind that old or nearly dried out pens are still valuable for rendering, as long as their pen points are sharp. These pens come in handy for fine-line detailing such as drawing features on a small face, doing crosshatching in tiny lace renderings, and rendering top stitching over fabric coloring. Be sure to distinguish the partly dried out pens from your new, wet pens. You can do this by taping the end of a dry pen on the side opposite the capped end. Even scotch tape twisted around a pen's barrel will identify it as your specialized tool.

Markers   Make a mental note or write down the types of marker tips you have and what kind of jobs you will need them for.

Keep marker lids on tight between uses. Listen for that "click" when you close them.

Keep the marker tips clean of other colors. Always clean any other color residue off your marker tips before you put them away.

Problem Solving   In this and the following chapters you will learn that often your rendering process will have to accommodate construction details. Almost every possible stripe, print, or texture will be affected by the types of construction you see on page 103. The more you know about different fabric construction treatments, the better you will be able to meet the challenge of rendering complex surfaces.

Get in the habit of using a sheet of tracing paper over your sketch to work out the altered progression of a stripe or print. This preliminary problem-solving step will save time in the long run by keeping you from making rendering mistakes on your all-important finished sketch.

Test Page

Ultrafine .005 pen stitch lines done after marker color.

⏱ *REMINDER*
Pen line drying time is 1 minute before coloring.

Ultrafine and fine points are best for small, tight areas and intricate detailing.

Brush tips are very flexible and great for loose, easy rendering.

A wedge nib can yield crisp angular coloring.

Thick broad nibs work for big areas such as wide shapes and background color.

Contoured nibs are good for all-around color and multipurpose rendering. These tips are the most versatile.

Darts

Tucks

Pin tucks

Side pleats Gores

Box pleat Cascade

Crystal pleats Cowl

Accordion pleats Godets

Mushroom pleats Flare

Smocking Ruffle

Shirring Pouf

Rendering Stripes

For all the differences between styles of stripes, awning to pin stripes, or poor boy to nautical, the method for rendering them is the same. It's all about spacing, planning, and size. What's the distance between each stripe? What kind of shape do the stripes go on? Where should you start on that shape? There are two answers to where to start. Either in the middle or at the bottom. The middle divides the space into sections. The bottom leaves you room to work your way up into the shape as you follow contours.

Starting in the middle of a shape divides the stripes over the center of your space. This helps you to see or identify angles, construction, or levels that need stripe definition, and it will enable you to determine contours, beyond just a linear grid.

MIDDLE

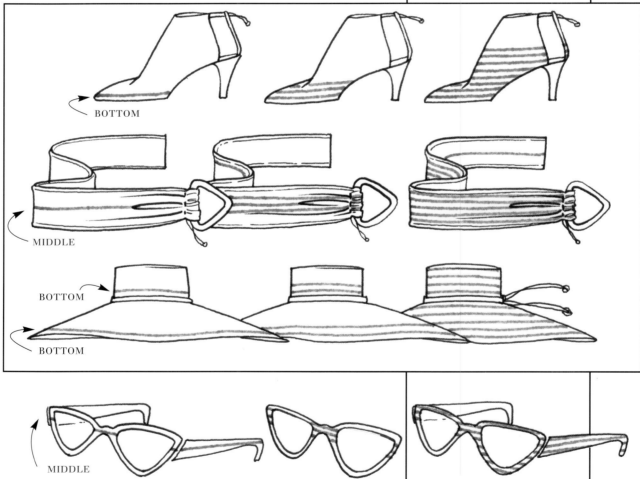

BOTTOM

MIDDLE

BOTTOM

BOTTOM

MIDDLE

STRIPES CAN CONFORM TO ALL
THE ANGLES IN A GIVEN SHAPE

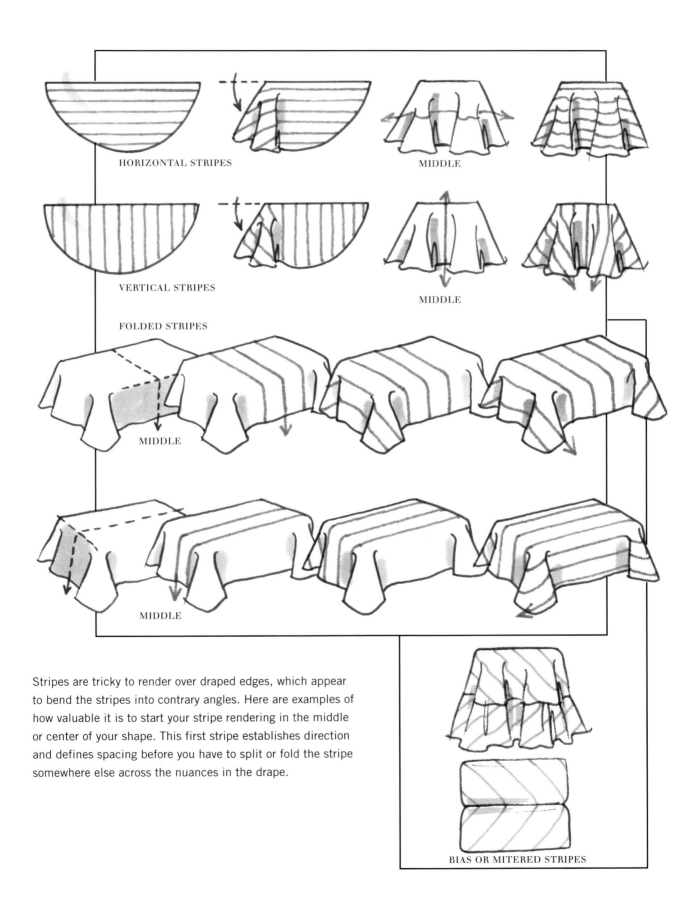

HORIZONTAL STRIPES

MIDDLE

VERTICAL STRIPES

MIDDLE

FOLDED STRIPES

MIDDLE

MIDDLE

Stripes are tricky to render over draped edges, which appear to bend the stripes into contrary angles. Here are examples of how valuable it is to start your stripe rendering in the middle or center of your shape. This first stripe establishes direction and defines spacing before you have to split or fold the stripe somewhere else across the nuances in the drape.

BIAS OR MITERED STRIPES

Horizontal Stripes

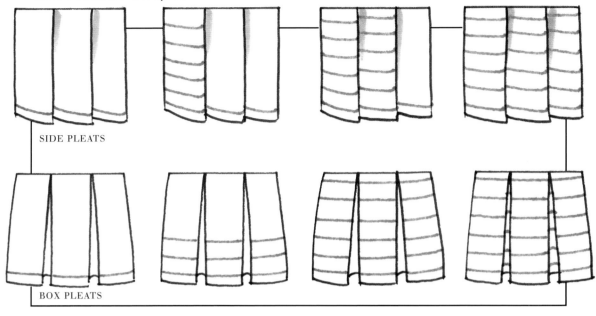

SIDE PLEATS

BOX PLEATS

VERTICAL AND HORIZONTAL MIDDLE
PLACEMENTS ARE DIFFERENT

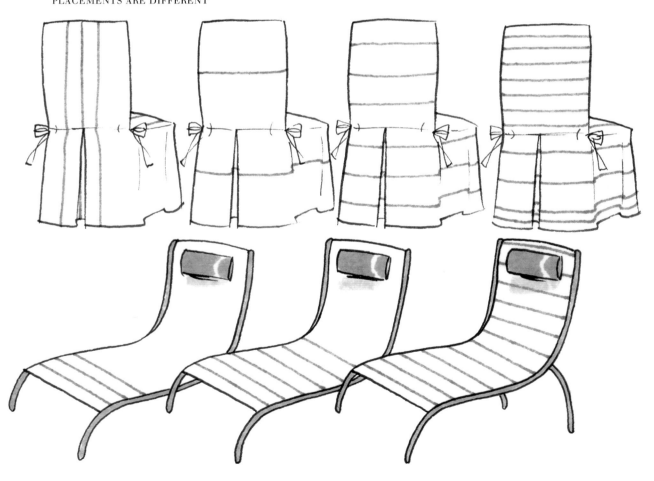

Vertical Stripes

SIDE PLEATS

KNIFE PLEATS

ACCORDION PLEATS

MUSHROOM PLEATS

BOX PLEATS

Stripe Behavior

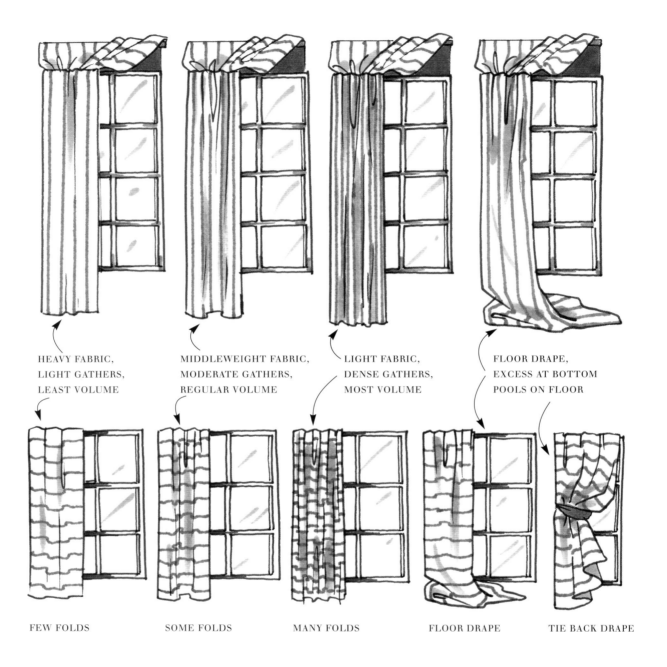

HEAVY FABRIC,
LIGHT GATHERS,
LEAST VOLUME

MIDDLEWEIGHT FABRIC,
MODERATE GATHERS,
REGULAR VOLUME

LIGHT FABRIC,
DENSE GATHERS,
MOST VOLUME

FLOOR DRAPE,
EXCESS AT BOTTOM
POOLS ON FLOOR

FEW FOLDS

SOME FOLDS

MANY FOLDS

FLOOR DRAPE

TIE BACK DRAPE

The rendering of stripes is affected by the fabric weight and the amount of fabric as much as by the construction detail. Notice the optical illusion as stripes are gathered together in bunches or rippling over folds. You can see that learning to render stripes will help you to render almost any print because after working on stripes, you've solved most of the rendering challenges that construction detailing can present.

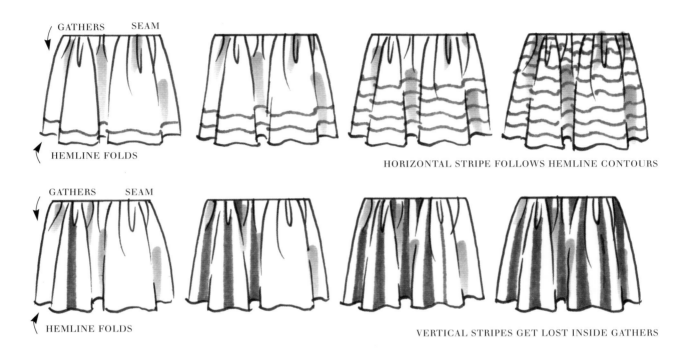

GATHERS   SEAM

HEMLINE FOLDS

HORIZONTAL STRIPE FOLLOWS HEMLINE CONTOURS

GATHERS   SEAM

HEMLINE FOLDS

VERTICAL STRIPES GET LOST INSIDE GATHERS

Contouring Stripes over a Form

Some contoured objects incorporate soft, rolling twists and turns that present very nuanced optical illusions of stripes and related prints. This kind of construction detail takes a bit of 4H pencil planning before you start using color. You can also work in sections or units, slowly completing complex areas before the more simple ones. This way you won't miss or mess up on a stripe's direction.

Stripes on Accessories

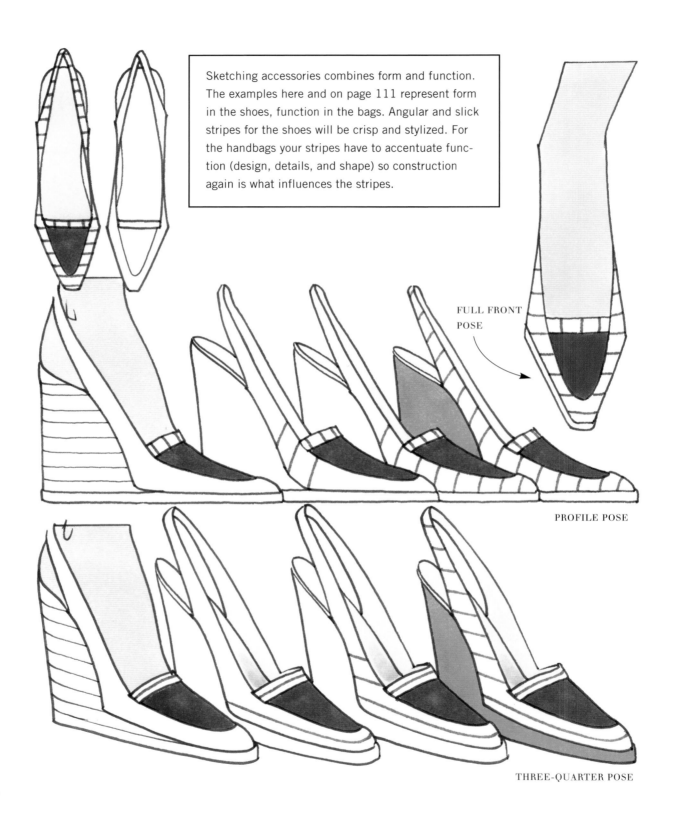

Sketching accessories combines form and function. The examples here and on page 111 represent form in the shoes, function in the bags. Angular and slick stripes for the shoes will be crisp and stylized. For the handbags your stripes have to accentuate function (design, details, and shape) so construction again is what influences the stripes.

FULL FRONT POSE

PROFILE POSE

THREE-QUARTER POSE

The design details in these bags are accentuated by outline, shading, and carefully nuanced stripe patterning.

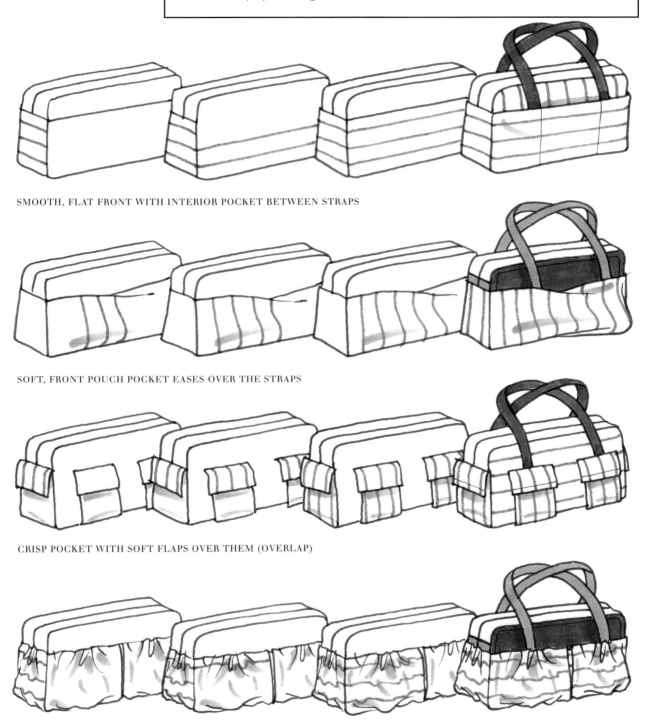

SMOOTH, FLAT FRONT WITH INTERIOR POCKET BETWEEN STRAPS

SOFT, FRONT POUCH POCKET EASES OVER THE STRAPS

CRISP POCKET WITH SOFT FLAPS OVER THEM (OVERLAP)

ELASTIC POCKETS WITH SOFT CRUSH LINES AND GATHERS

Fashion Stripes

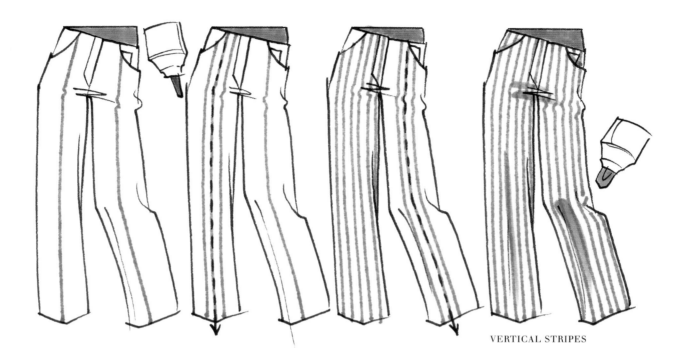

VERTICAL STRIPES

The rendering techniques that apply to accessories and home furnishings apply to striped clothing as well. Vertical stripes start in the middle of a shape, and horizontal stripes can be centered or can start across the bottom. Fashion puts the bottom stripe across the hemline, which has the most impact on a stripe's directions.

- **Vertical:** Posed garments create body angles to follow.
- **Horizontal:** Pose is still important but hemline takes precedence.
- **Bias stripes:** A challenge to follow the grain line in the fabric as well as the construction detail.
- **Engineered or mitered:** For this work in stripes you need to read the design seams. Carefully plot out the cut and line up the stripes at those seams.

MITERED STRIPES

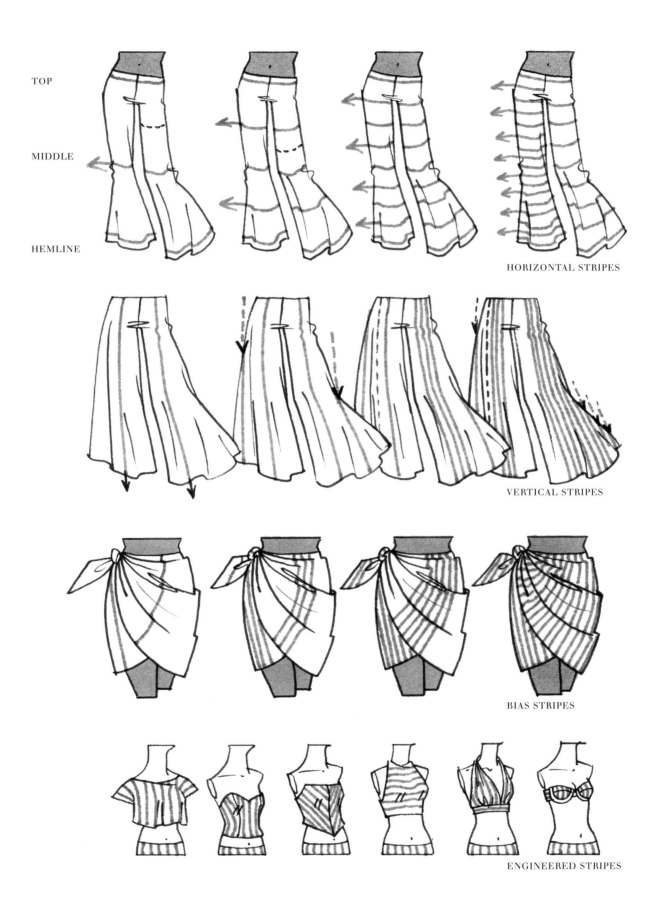

TOP

MIDDLE

HEMLINE

HORIZONTAL STRIPES

VERTICAL STRIPES

BIAS STRIPES

ENGINEERED STRIPES

Stripes as the Basis
of Print Development

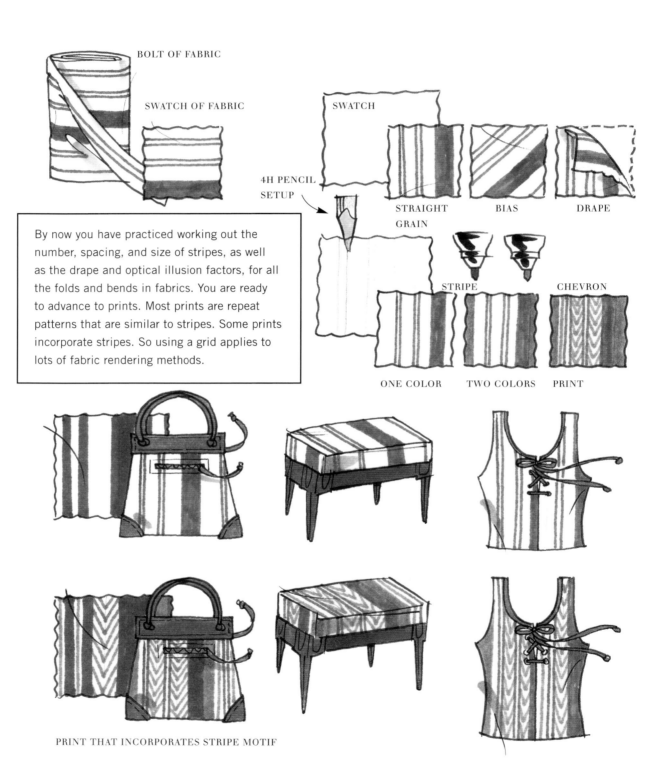

BOLT OF FABRIC

SWATCH OF FABRIC

SWATCH

4H PENCIL SETUP

STRAIGHT GRAIN **BIAS** **DRAPE**

STRIPE **CHEVRON**

ONE COLOR **TWO COLORS** **PRINT**

By now you have practiced working out the number, spacing, and size of stripes, as well as the drape and optical illusion factors, for all the folds and bends in fabrics. You are ready to advance to prints. Most prints are repeat patterns that are similar to stripes. Some prints incorporate stripes. So using a grid applies to lots of fabric rendering methods.

PRINT THAT INCORPORATES STRIPE MOTIF

Prints on a Grid — Color-on-Color Jacquard

- Begin with a solid, flat background using the scrub technique for smooth color rendering.
- Start the grid, using a darker shade of the same color, in the middle, and then move across and down the center in even spaces.
- Drop the repeat pattern consistently inside each unit within the grid.

Stripe-Based Print — Like an Ikat or Southwestern Print

- Map out the direction for the print based on the stripe and the visible seams that affect the cut of the material.
- For multicolor prints start with either the dominant color or the lightest color.
- After completing the stripe portion of the print (easy part), fill in the rest of the repeat pattern (hard part) between the stripes.

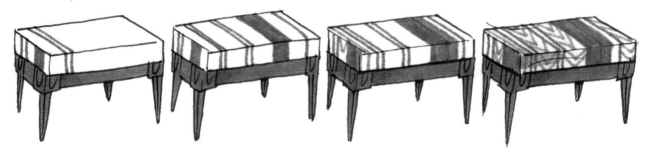

Grid on an Angle — Argyle Knit Print

- Lightly pencil in the grid on a diagonal so that the lines create diamond shapes instead of boxes.
- Fill in the alternating rows of diamond shapes. Use color as if it were ribbing—in neat little close rows.
- Create another diagonal grid in (ribbed) line, which goes on top of or over the color diamonds.

2B PENCIL, KNIT GRID

2B PENCIL KNIT ROWS

Moving into Geometric Prints

Polka Dots

Most (but not all) polka dots are an even print, set out on a grid, with the dots equidistant from each other. So you can easily map out the print for any size dot.

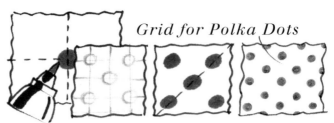

Grid for Polka Dots

Fine-point tip for smaller dots

Buffalo Checks

This checkerboard print is also on a grid. Again, make each square the same size and also equidistant from each other in alternating rows.

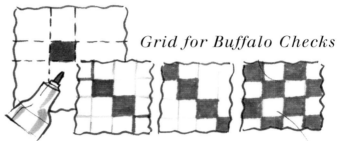

Grid for Buffalo Checks

Fine-point tip to outline boxes so you can color in the checkerboard print without getting lost in the grid.

Ginghams

You can call this print stripes in two directions, or a color banded grid. After you complete the bands, down and across each other, go back and make their centers (where they overlap) darker.

Grid for Ginghams

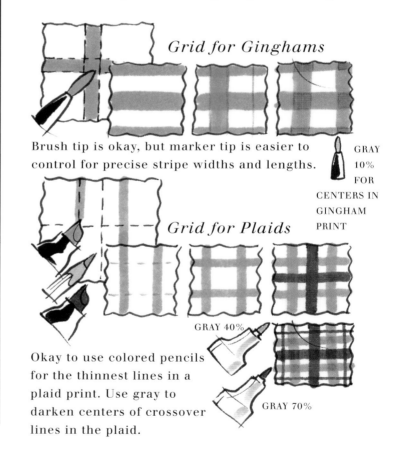

Brush tip is okay, but marker tip is easier to control for precise stripe widths and lengths.

GRAY 10% FOR CENTERS IN GINGHAM PRINT

Plaids

Plaids sometimes look like multicolor grids. The spacing may vary, but plaid is still layers of lines down and across each other. As in rendering ginghams, you need to go back into the print to darken the centers where one color crosses over another, which produces a third value.

Grid for Plaids

Okay to use colored pencils for the thinnest lines in a plaid print. Use gray to darken centers of crossover lines in the plaid.

GRAY 40%

GRAY 70%

Argyle/
Harlequin Print

Diagonal grid creates diamond shapes. You have to plan the grid so that the print will work on the pose to get the boxes even on both sides.

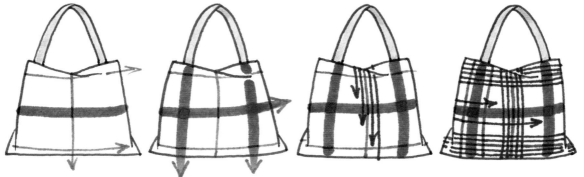

Simple Plaid

Plan the grid across the middle of the surface you have to render. Work in layers of colors (use a pen for fine lines). Consider working in one direction or one color at a time.

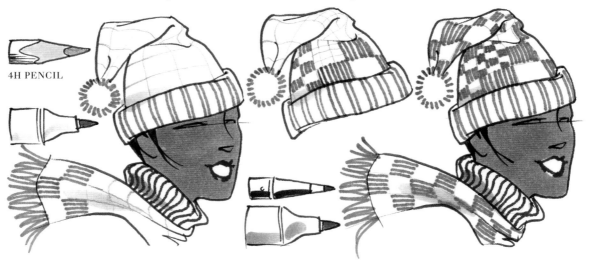

4H PENCIL

Geometric Print

Remember that all knit prints can be rendered in rows to reflect knit ribbing. Plan out the print in a 4H pencil, so that the print can be contoured to fit into the shape.

Challenges of Geometric Prints

Perspective can add to your rendering problems. It brings in certain angles that add to the form and construction for possible optical illusions in prints. A boxy chair will usually change the print because of the perspective between the back and the seat. Notice how the checkerboard print flattens out across the seat. On the other more rounded chair you've got a normally rigid gingham print rolling around and bending into spirals over the arm of this chair. On page 119 is a plaid that seems to constantly change direction between the drape and fold in the coverlet.

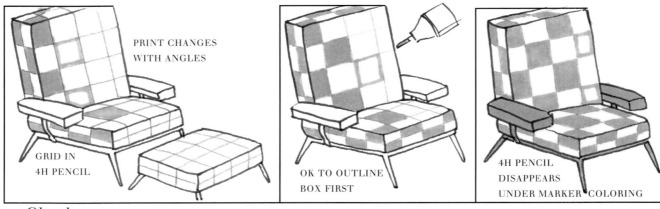

PRINT CHANGES WITH ANGLES

GRID IN 4H PENCIL

OK TO OUTLINE BOX FIRST

4H PENCIL DISAPPEARS UNDER MARKER COLORING

Checks

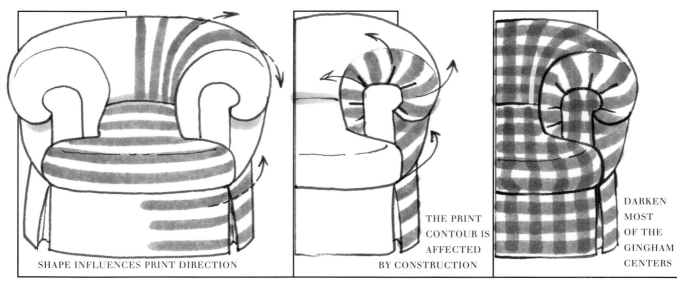

SHAPE INFLUENCES PRINT DIRECTION

THE PRINT CONTOUR IS AFFECTED BY CONSTRUCTION

DARKEN MOST OF THE GINGHAM CENTERS

Gingham

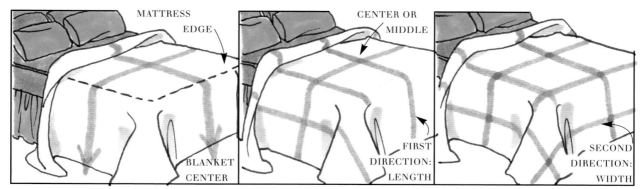

Windowpane

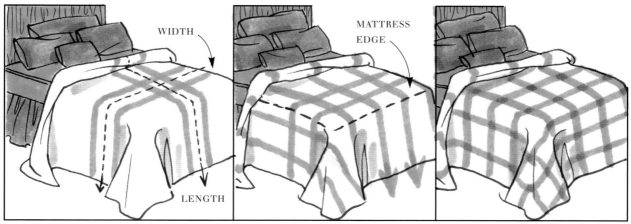

Gingham

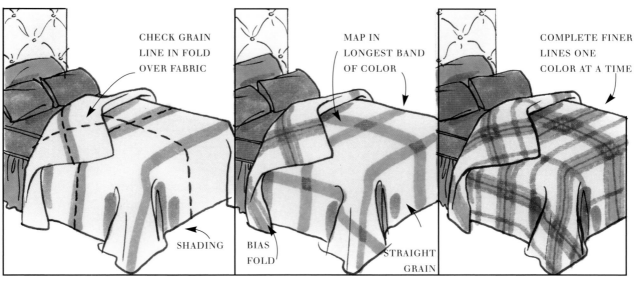

Plaid

Reducing Prints

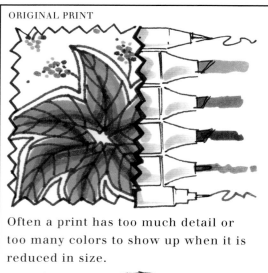

ORIGINAL PRINT

Often a print has too much detail or too many colors to show up when it is reduced in size.

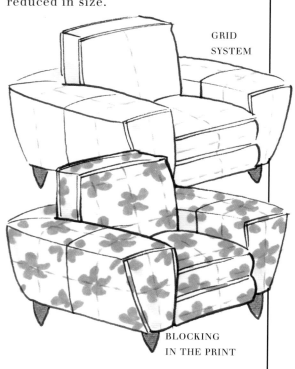

GRID SYSTEM

BLOCKING IN THE PRINT

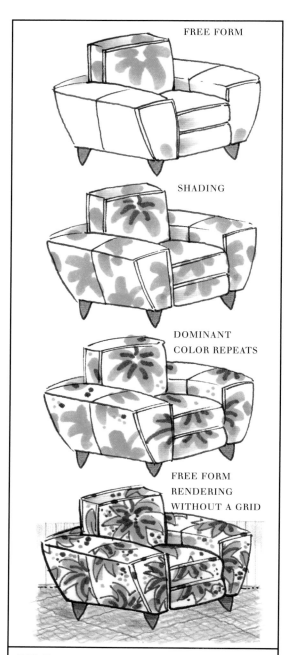

FREE FORM

SHADING

DOMINANT COLOR REPEATS

FREE FORM RENDERING WITHOUT A GRID

Grid System

If you need to follow the original print sequence of your fabric, block out or use a grid to map out the repeat.

Without a Grid

This technique is for loose, quick rendering. Start your print with random repeats of the largest (dominant) component (in the repeat) of your fabric print.

You will have to use your judgment in rendering fabrics with too many colors or too much detail for it all to fit into a small sketch. Look to re-create the color story and the print feel in an abbreviated style.

START
WITH
SHADOWS

GRAY 50% SHADING
CREATES DEPTH
IN FOLDS

DROP IN MAJOR
COLOR FOR PRINT
PLACEMENT

ADD THE
ABBREVIATED
PRINT FOR PARTIAL
RENDERING

USE GRAVITY TO
PULL YOUR PRINT
DOWN OVER THE
FABRIC—DENSE
PRINT AT THE TOP
CASCADING DOWN
INTO LESS AND LESS
COLOR

In addition to tight and loose rendering, there is also partial rendering. As in this example, most of the work on the pattern is done for the major design element of curtain draping over the rod. The rendering starts to taper off over the rest of the drapery that is falling behind the chair. You always pick and choose where a partial rendering would be appropriate. For instance, where would it be most or least important to see this print in your sketch?

Fashion Prints

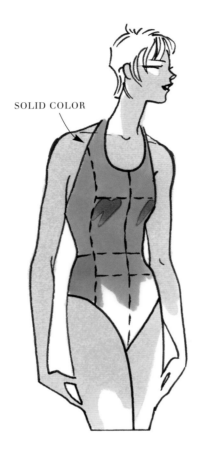

SOLID COLOR

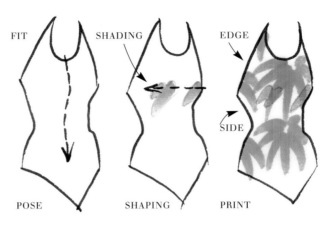

FIT   SHADING   EDGE

SIDE

POSE   SHAPING   PRINT

Print

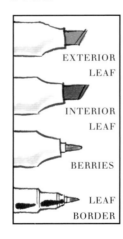

EXTERIOR LEAF

INTERIOR LEAF

BERRIES

LEAF BORDER

In order for a print to look like it fits across a body or on the flat of a garment, the rendering has to touch a few sides or edges to suggest that it's going "around" the form, even in a partial or loose technique. The part of the print going over or around the edges disappears to suggest shaping contours and to suggest that the print continues on the side and back of the garment. This method brings out the fit of the print as well as the fit of the garment, whatever your style of drawing.

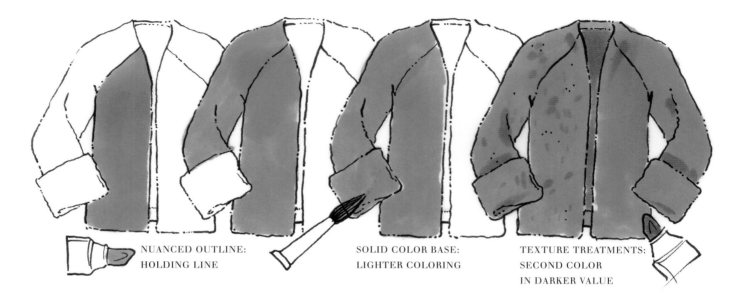

NUANCED OUTLINE:
HOLDING LINE

SOLID COLOR BASE:
LIGHTER COLORING

TEXTURE TREATMENTS:
SECOND COLOR
IN DARKER VALUE

The choice is yours as to which to render first in a multifabric sketch, the easier solid color or the print, which is harder.

The top row shows you how to do a tight, finished rendering for a solid color that has a subtle surface texture like terry cloth.

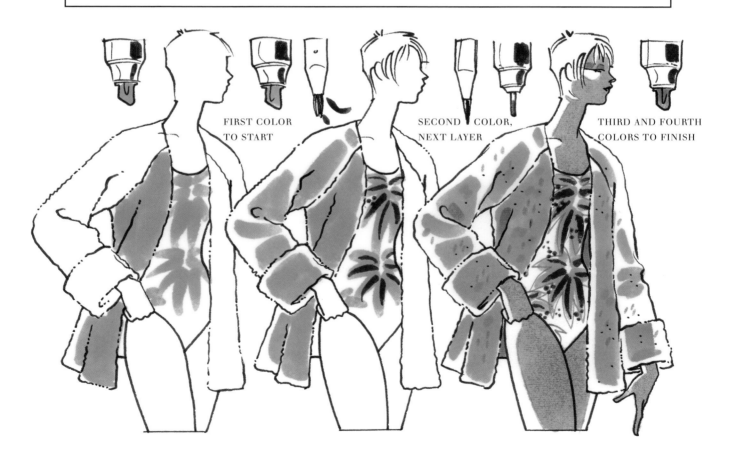

FIRST COLOR
TO START

SECOND COLOR,
NEXT LAYER

THIRD AND FOURTH
COLORS TO FINISH

Outline and Color with Fabric Mixes

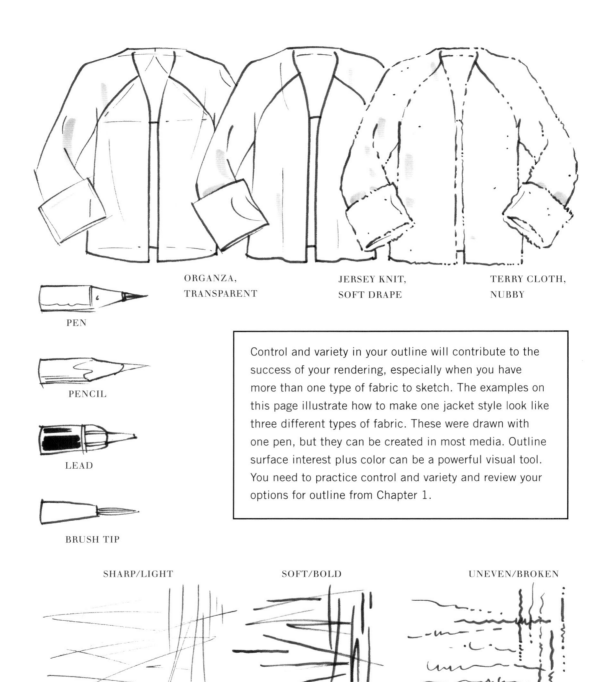

ORGANZA,
TRANSPARENT

JERSEY KNIT,
SOFT DRAPE

TERRY CLOTH,
NUBBY

PEN

PENCIL

LEAD

BRUSH TIP

Control and variety in your outline will contribute to the
success of your rendering, especially when you have
more than one type of fabric to sketch. The examples on
this page illustrate how to make one jacket style look like
three different types of fabric. These were drawn with
one pen, but they can be created in most media. Outline
surface interest plus color can be a powerful visual tool.
You need to practice control and variety and review your
options for outline from Chapter 1.

SHARP/LIGHT

SOFT/BOLD

UNEVEN/BROKEN

OUTLINE USED FOR THE
ORGANZA JACKET'S
TRANSPARENCY

OUTLINE USED FOR
THE JERSEY KNIT
JACKET'S SOFT DRAPE

OUTLINE USED FOR THE LOOPS
AND SURFACE TEXTURE IN THE
TERRY CLOTH JACKET

NIB OR BRUSH
PEN

FABRIC

FLESH
TONE
#1

TWO-TONE
FLESH

BODY
#2

#1

OPTION OF MARKER
OR PENCIL

FABRIC

FLESH TONE #2

INSIDE BACK OF JACKET

LINES IN TRANSPARENT FABRIC

SMOOTH

NUBBY TWO-TONE

PENCIL
OR PEN
OUTLINE

FLAT / SOLID

SHINY

SEMITRANSPARENT

SOLID AND TRANSPARENT
PANELED FABRICS

DOUBLE LAYER,
ONE FABRIC OVER ANOTHER

Options in Rendering Prints

BACKGROUND FIRST

DOMINANT COLOR FIRST

PRINT FIRST

Here are three different methods for working on a multicolor, repeat print:

Background First
After you pencil in the dominant shapes of your print, surround them with your background color.

Dominant or Lightest Color First
If the lightest color is the lead or has the most coverage in your print, start with that color in your rendering. This prevents possible smearing as lighter colors have problems going over darker.

Print First
Pencil in the repeat so that you will know how much to fill in with the (probable) dominant color in the repeat.

Print Planning
When you have to combine fabrics in a sketch, you may want to choose which to do first—the easier solid or the more difficult print. Either way, get your shading done first.

Print Layout
Every print has a layout that you use to plot out or plan out your rendering layers. With certain types of construction the fabric's grain line will influence your print's layout.

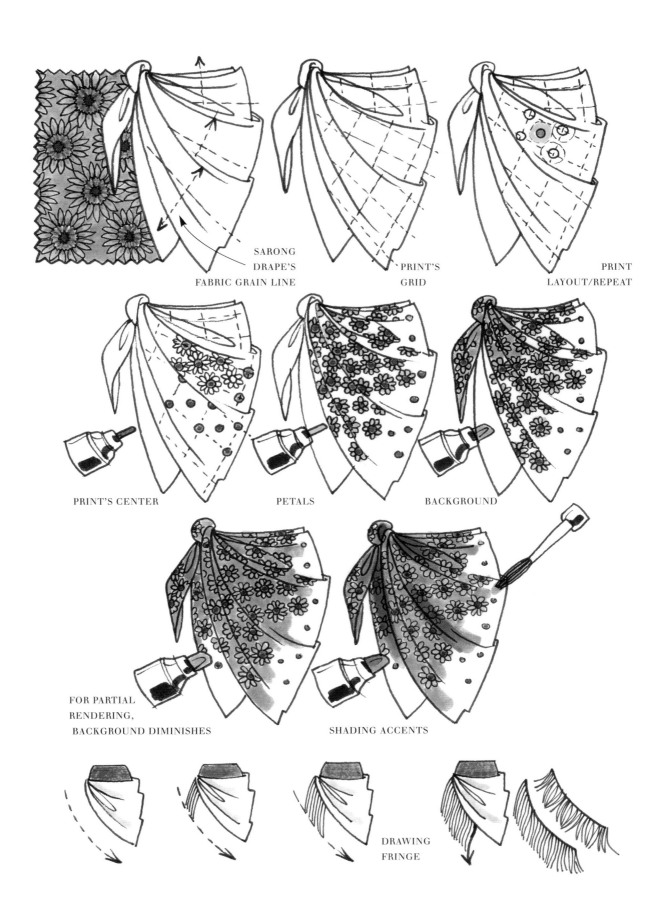

SARONG DRAPE'S
FABRIC GRAIN LINE

PRINT'S
GRID

PRINT
LAYOUT/REPEAT

PRINT'S CENTER

PETALS

BACKGROUND

FOR PARTIAL
RENDERING,
BACKGROUND DIMINISHES

SHADING ACCENTS

DRAWING
FRINGE

Prints for Croquis

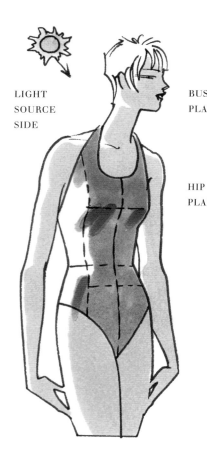

LIGHT
SOURCE
SIDE

BUST
PLANE

HIP
PLANE

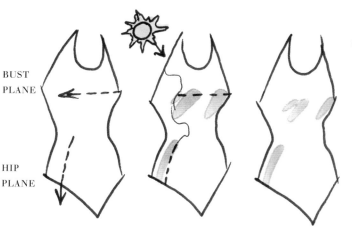

CONTOURED
SHADING
GIVES THE
IMPRESSION
OF BODY
SHAPING
AND ADDS
DIMENSION
TO THE
GARMENT
ON THE
FIGURE

Partial Print Rendering

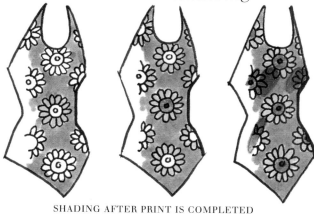

SHADING AFTER PRINT IS COMPLETED

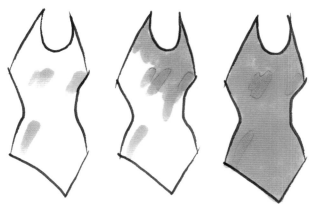

SHADING BEFORE SOLID COLOR BASE

Review

Shading must reflect the curves in the figure regardless of the light source or whether it appears in a partial rendering.

For *partial rendering*, you work with both the light source side and the figure contours to keep the coloring loose on a pose.

Partial rendering for flats needs to be consistent. Choose one direction or side for the print or color to fade away.

SHADING FOR FLATS

LIGHT
SOURCE
SIDE

SHADING TIPS

CONTOURS

FOLDS

DRAPE

SOLID BLUE GETS
GRAY 40% SHAD-
OWS

SOLID YELLOW
GETS GRAY 40%
SHADOWS

PRINT GETS GRAY
70% SHADOWS

FIGURE
PROPORTIONS
FOR FLATS

Tight Rendering for Prints

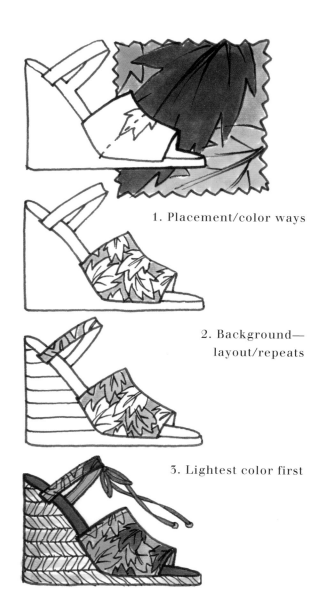

1. Placement/color ways

2. Background—
layout/repeats

3. Lightest color first

4. Completing nonprint details

Some prints have such a specific pattern or color story that you will want to do a finished or tight rendering. For a tight rendering, make sure to center the print or place the pattern precisely in your sketch to maximize the pattern's repeat and the dominant colors.

Draw the lead element or major feature in the print on the center or over the most prominent part of the shape you have to render.

Stay true to the layout or grid work in the print. If it's oversized, try to accommodate as many of the pattern's motifs as possible.

It is easier to go from light to dark color rather than vice versa.

Once you have completed the print's major motifs or colors, you can finish the other design elements that are included in the image. This way if you have to start over because of a goof, you haven't wasted time on the easy stuff.

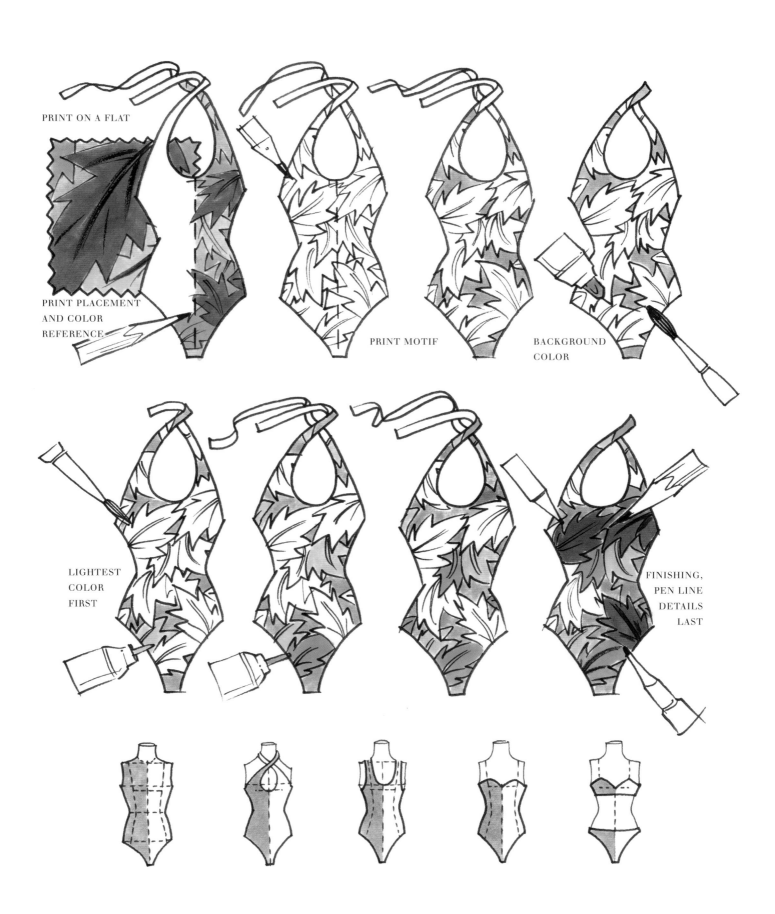

PRINT ON A FLAT

PRINT PLACEMENT
AND COLOR
REFERENCE

PRINT MOTIF

BACKGROUND
COLOR

LIGHTEST
COLOR
FIRST

FINISHING,
PEN LINE
DETAILS
LAST

Partial Rendering for Prints

Base Layer for Prints

Partial or loose rendering for a multicolor print can start with the base layer or a solid color background. This way the print over the loose layer background color is impressionistic, as opposed to being copied exactly. It keeps the rendering look fresh and spontaneous.

BASE: LIME GREEN,
TIGHT/SOLID

BASE: LIME GREEN,
LOSE/PARTIAL

Camouflage Print

With a partial or loose background color underneath the print, you learn to keep that print just a bit less than or slightly over the base color. This keeps it from looking rigid or like a cardboard cutout.

SECOND LAYER: OLIVE GREEN OVER
LOOSE/PARTIAL BACKGROUND COLOR

THIRD LAYER: BURNT UMBER
FOURTH LAYER: SHADING/GRAY 70%

Paisley Print

Paisley prints can get extremely complex with difficult coloring to follow, especially in reduction on a sketch. Unless you are into fabric design, you usually do not have to be completely faithful to a print as long as you can convey the gist of it in your rendering. Tiny bits of lighter colors going over darker colors are difficult to do, but pens usually can go over marker colors.

Paisley Print — Loose Interpretation

PRINT REPEAT OR LAYOUT

SPACING

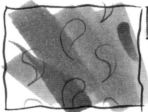

BASE AND SHADOW

BACKGROUND

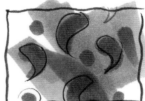

MAJOR PRINT DETAIL

DOMINANT COLOR

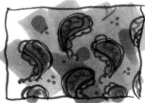

FINE LINE DETAILS

MAJOR MOTIF

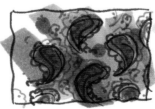 

SMALLEST ACCENT DETAIL

FINISHING TOUCHES

Prints for Eyewear

Metallic eyeglass frames may be popular now, but as trends come and go, there are retro or edgy looks in plastic frames. They often imitate natural prints. (See rendering for metallics in Chapter 6.)

Most prints can be reduced to three easy steps, starting with a solid base color. The middle step usually establishes the color variations in the print. The finish or last step is for smaller, nuanced detailing.

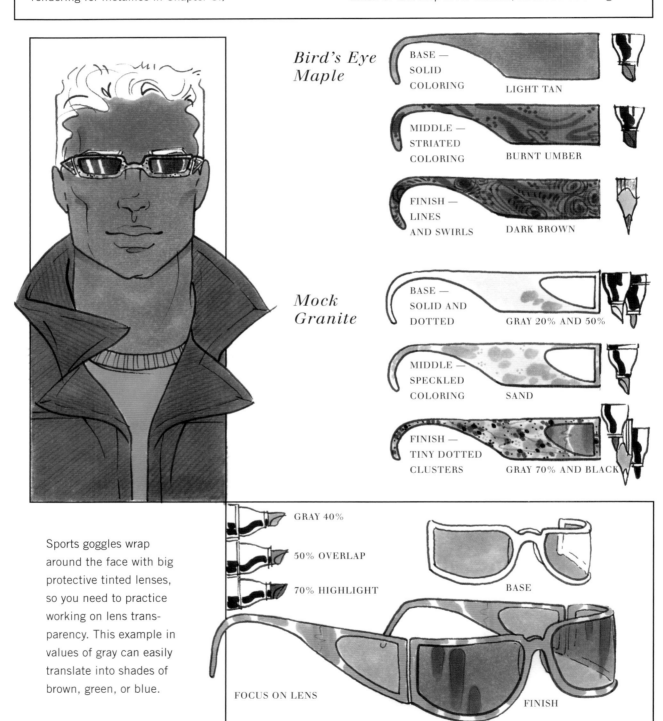

Bird's Eye Maple

BASE — SOLID COLORING   LIGHT TAN

MIDDLE — STRIATED COLORING   BURNT UMBER

FINISH — LINES AND SWIRLS   DARK BROWN

Mock Granite

BASE — SOLID AND DOTTED   GRAY 20% AND 50%

MIDDLE — SPECKLED COLORING   SAND

FINISH — TINY DOTTED CLUSTERS   GRAY 70% AND BLACK

Sports goggles wrap around the face with big protective tinted lenses, so you need to practice working on lens transparency. This example in values of gray can easily translate into shades of brown, green, or blue.

GRAY 40%

50% OVERLAP

70% HIGHLIGHT

BASE

FOCUS ON LENS

FINISH

Mock Tortoise Shell

Base: Solid coloring, scrub technique
Middle: Striated coloring, chunks and dashes
Finish: Dabs of color, irregular dots

Faux Horn

Base: Angled striated color, no solid background
Middle: Grainy pencil lines, irregular lines
Finish: Deeper thicker lines, same angles

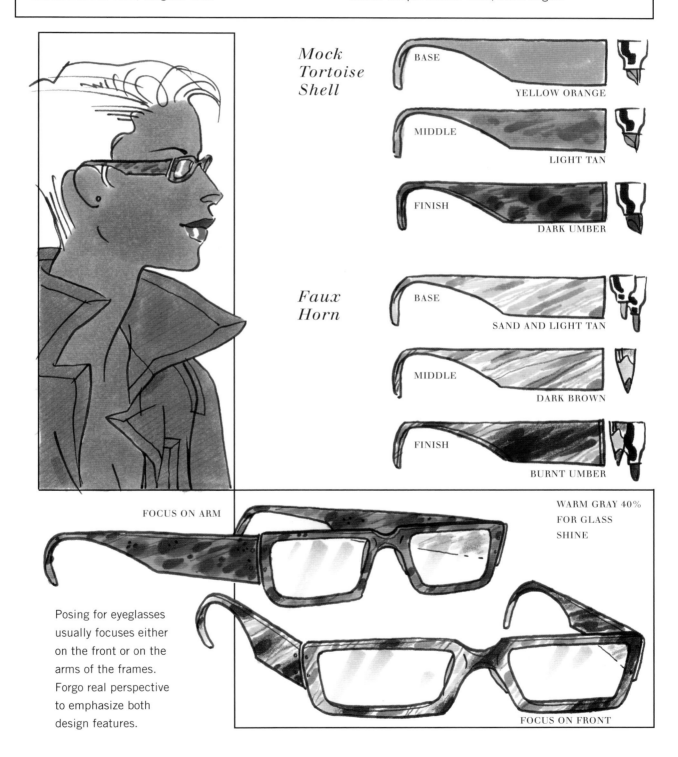

Mock Tortoise Shell

BASE — YELLOW ORANGE

MIDDLE — LIGHT TAN

FINISH — DARK UMBER

Faux Horn

BASE — SAND AND LIGHT TAN

MIDDLE — DARK BROWN

FINISH — BURNT UMBER

FOCUS ON ARM

WARM GRAY 40% FOR GLASS SHINE

Posing for eyeglasses usually focuses either on the front or on the arms of the frames. Forgo real perspective to emphasize both design features.

FOCUS ON FRONT

Assignment

Gridded prints, like checks, ginghams, and plaids, are halfway between stripes and full-blown prints. The prints on a grid are a good place to start practicing. This is enough of a challenge without being overwhelming for a beginner.

Work out four easy shapes. Start with a simple box, of equal sides, to create a checkerboard pattern. With that completed, draw out three shapes, one for fashion, one for accessories, and one for home fashion. Focus on shape or construction as a means to develop your skills in rendering prints across, over, around, and into construction details. For more challenging practice try to draw and render these prints onto some of the bend, fold, and roll of draped fabric that incorporates some of the more difficult optical illusions for an illustrator, again on items for fashion, accessories, and home fashion.

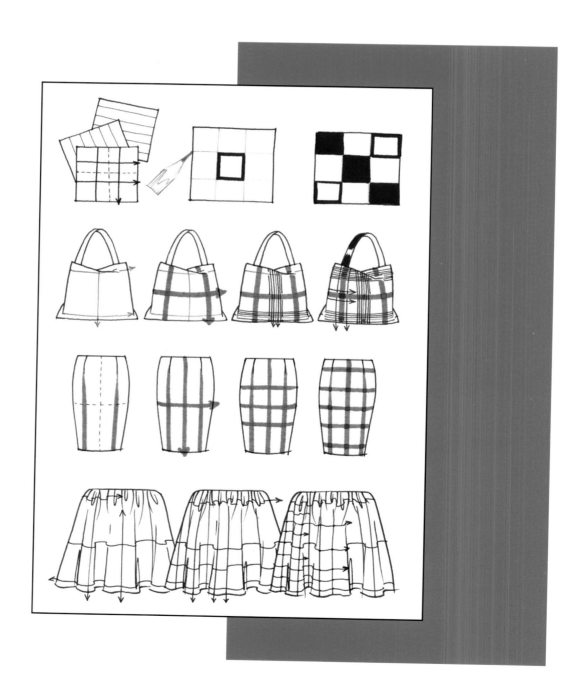

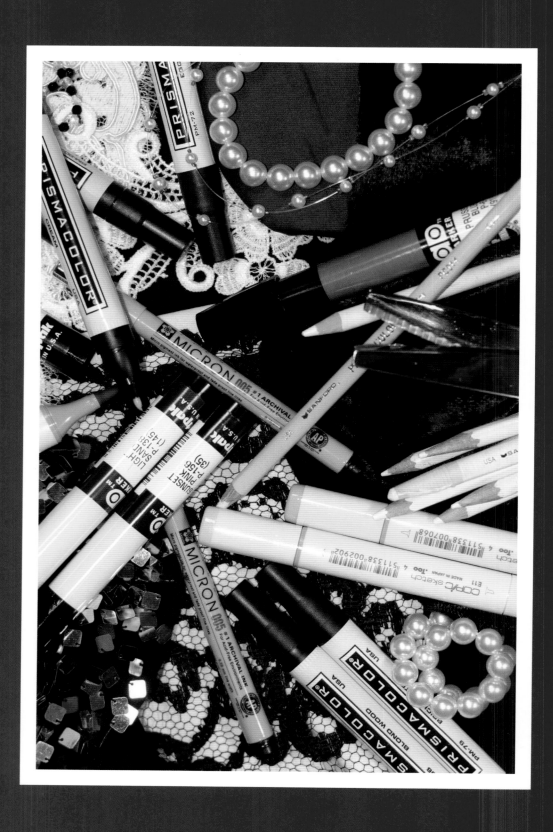

LIGHT AND DARK COLORS

CHAPTER 6

Markers and Pens

Markers

There is a fabulous range available of pastel colors in markers in every brand. Their color charts are the best indicator of actual tints, but it is hard to determine color from the label on the marker itself. That's why you should always bring a snip of the kind of paper you will be rendering on with you to the store, to use as a test strip so you can get an accurate view of the color before you buy that marker.

For the lightest pastels, look for names of their hues listed on page 141—iced, cool, frost, baby powdery, pale. Words like these indicate a lightly tinted color.

Marker usually dries a bit lighter than it looks during application.

Rendering in layers for pastel solids will definitely make the color darker.

Shadowy grays come in lighter values, grays to 10% and 20%, which can be used for shading pastels.

The range in darker colors is not as broad as in the pastels. To deepen a color or to get it "dustier" or toned down, add deep gray 80%.

Metallic Markers and Pens

Metallic pens or markers usually have to be shaken before they are used. Be careful because they can splatter.

Keep all metallic marker and pen caps snugly closed and possibly in an airtight plastic container or a resealable plastic bag. This will keep them from drying out or clogging up too quickly (but not indefinitely).

Pens

Thinner, delicate, fine-line pen points make great outlines for pastel colors. Thicker, bolder, heavy-line pen points can stand up to dark marker coloring.

This is where old pens and old markers come into play. Old pens may make feathery thin lines that could create a texture.

Colored Pens

Colored pens are a major asset. In addition to the fine tip on your double-ended markers, colored pens usually offer the thinnest line of color possible. Gel pens offer the widest selection of pastel colors. Other types of colored pens offer bolder, darker lines that can easily stand up to dark marker coloring. Colored pens also make a colorful alternative to the usual black outline in your sketches.

Just as with markers, remember to snap or click covers tightly on the pens and keep the pens away from any heat source that can dry them out. Too much pressure on pen tips can cause them to clog or can fray the tips. Careful use will preserve them for longer. The jury is still out about which direction to store pens—standing tip up, standing tip down, or lying flat. Some store them tip up so ink won't blob at the tip. Others store them tip down so the tip won't dry out. Storing them lying down seems to solve both problems, so maybe that is the best way for colored pens to last longer.

Test Page

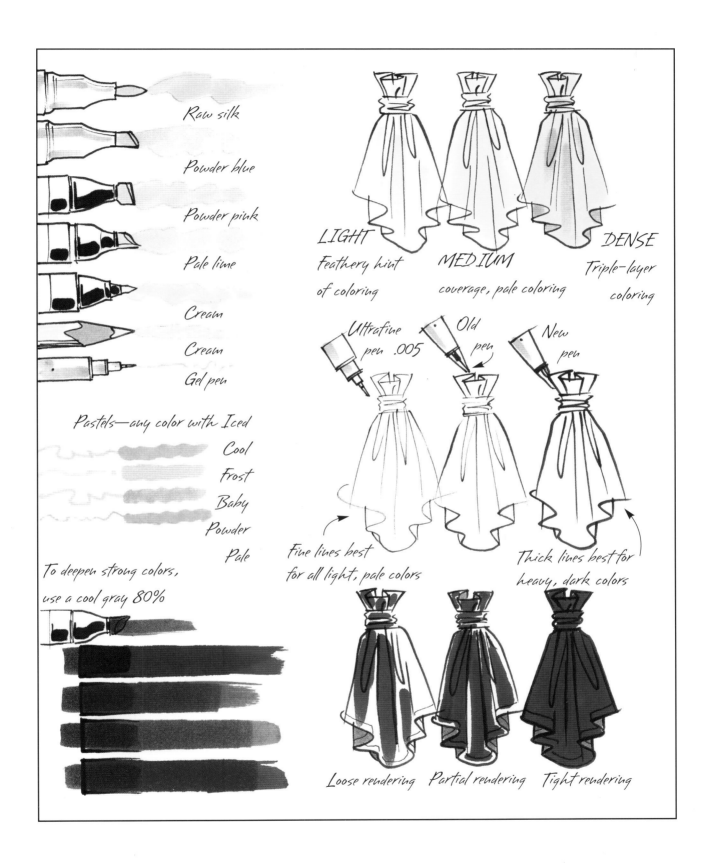

Raw silk

Powder blue

Powder pink

Pale lime

Cream

Cream

Gel pen

Pastels—any color with Iced

Cool

Frost

Baby

Powder

Pale

To deepen strong colors,
use a cool gray 80%

LIGHT
Feathery hint
of coloring

MEDIUM
coverage, pale coloring

DENSE
Triple-layer
coloring

Ultrafine
pen .005

Old
pen

New
pen

Fine lines best
for all light, pale colors

Thick lines best for
heavy, dark colors

Loose rendering   Partial rendering   Tight rendering

Fall/Winter Creams and Whites

SUEDE

KNIT

TAN

EGGSHELL

CREME

PENCIL POINT

PENCIL SIDE

PUTTY

GRAY 30%

2B PENCIL

FLANNEL

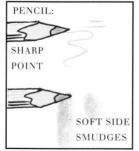

PENCIL:

SHARP POINT

SOFT SIDE SMUDGES

Pastels used for the winter colors and fabrics are usually a mix of textures in varying degrees of smooth and rough; for example, suede to shearling or brushed cotton flannels or chunky knits, as illustrated here. Pencils are an essential rendering tool for these subtle, or not so subtle, surface interest fabrics that have to appear heavy and warm.

Spring/Summer Creams and Whites

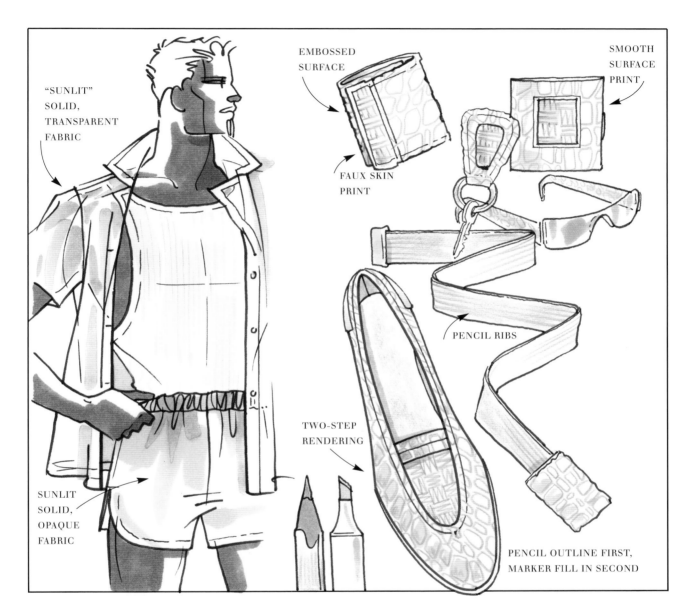

"SUNLIT" SOLID, TRANSPARENT FABRIC

EMBOSSED SURFACE

SMOOTH SURFACE PRINT

FAUX SKIN PRINT

PENCIL RIBS

TWO-STEP RENDERING

SUNLIT SOLID, OPAQUE FABRIC

PENCIL OUTLINE FIRST, MARKER FILL IN SECOND

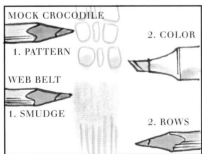

MOCK CROCODILE

1. PATTERN

2. COLOR

WEB BELT

1. SMUDGE

2. ROWS

Summer weight clothing and accessories are often illustrated as "sunlit," and they are often created as partial or loose renderings. Rendering is supposed to look cool, airy, and lightweight in "breezy" colors. Quite often you will be using pencil first and marker second for some of the buttery, soft surface interest pastels.

Bridal Rendering

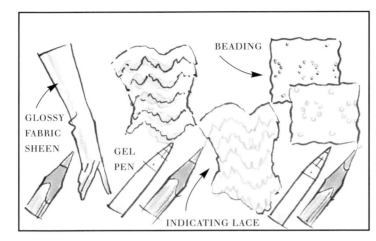

Bridal fashions offer the added challenges of rendering intricate, delicate laces, beading, and ribboning, not to mention all sorts of exquisite tulles and other translucent fabrics.

Often the main attraction is the bridal veil in some form of tulle. It has to appear see-through, and yet convey a bit of a graininess. Here you put the marker peek-a-boo colors on before adding the grainy smudges in colored pencil over it.

Accessories like gloves or bags need only a hint of color, if they accompany a figure, because they shouldn't take attention away from the gown.

Bodices with intricate seaming or lace may affect the outline contours or need color emphasis on detailing and construction.

Beading is a challenge because it signifies both a pattern and a raised surface, so you may have to add some pencil shading near the colors to give the beads a "lift."

TULLE BRIDAL VEIL IN COLORED PENCILS

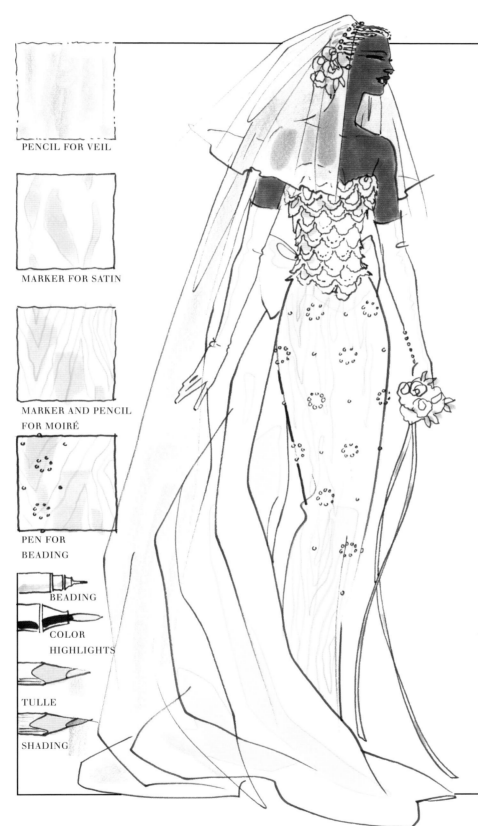

PENCIL FOR VEIL

MARKER FOR SATIN

MARKER AND PENCIL
FOR MOIRÉ

PEN FOR
BEADING

BEADING

COLOR
HIGHLIGHTS

TULLE

SHADING

Bridal Looks

All wedding gowns present a glamour image and the rendering challenge of maximizing the glamour quotient yet minimizing the rendering in keeping with all the subtle nuances in the bridal look.

Tulle

Keep it translucent by suggesting that it is see-through. Suggest volume or layers by keeping the color minimal and the lines crisp.

Lace

Depending on the size of your sketch or figure, the lace should be in small increments of loose or partial rendering so that it appears light, fine, and delicate.

Taffeta, Silk, Satin

There may be subtle prints or patterns to render. For these you probably will use pencil to make the print look delicate. Gel pens can also be light colors, but their ink line can look heavy on these types of fabrics.

Beading

The best you can do is get some "lift" by using the heavier pen lines for beads or sequins in contrast to the feathery pencil patterns.

Bridal sketches can be very pale. The use of a related or contrast color as a backdrop behind the figure is a useful device to accentuate the paleness, emphasize subtle detail, and maximize shape.

OPTIONS

SHARP
EXTRA
FINE
POINTS

TULLE VEIL

HINT OF
FLESHTONE

MOIRÉ
TAFFETA

LACE OVER
CHIFFON
LAYERS

ICE BLUES

PALE MISTS

HARD PENCIL TIPS

BABY PINKS

SHERBET COLORS

WHITE-ON-WHITE FABRICS

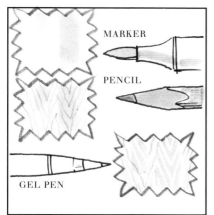

MARKER

PENCIL

GEL PEN

DETAILING LAYERS

PENCIL
SIDE

PENCIL
POINT

TULLE VEIL, PENCIL

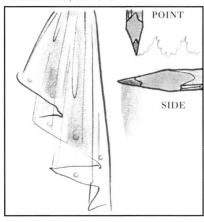

POINT

SIDE

White-on-White Fabrics

Cool whites can get baby blue highlights. Warm whites can get cream or subtle pink highlights. For a cool white you can set a strong blue background to accentuate the pale blue highlights. To render the print on a "white," put light blue pencil on the white of the paper and white pencil (or pen) over the blue highlights, as shown in the example at the top left.

Layers

Often there are multiple layers in a mix of fabrics cascading over each other at the hem of the gown. Use a combination of pen line and pencil line to represent the overlapping layers.

Details

Things like the hemline "pooling" or trailing across the floor are drawing tricks, as illustrated here. Circle your line from the front hem over and around to the line of the side of the dress to create the gown's train.

BROAD TIP: EDGING, HARD/FLAT
BRUSH TIP: DRAPE, SOFT/EXPRESSIVE

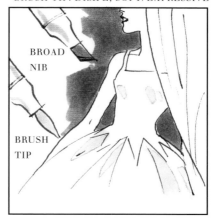

BROAD
NIB

BRUSH
TIP

TRAIN FOR GOWN

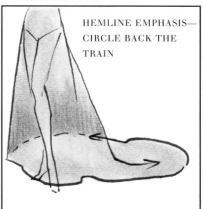

HEMLINE EMPHASIS—
CIRCLE BACK THE
TRAIN

COLOR FOR TRAIN

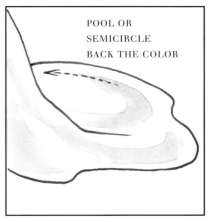

POOL OR
SEMICIRCLE
BACK THE COLOR

Iridescent Colors

Iridescent details are often tiny, yet critical, design features that illustrate pearls, buttons, or gemstones. Also beading and sequins need to look as glamorous as any fabric or lace details. The more emphasis or nuance that you can render on these, the more luxe or expensive they will look, adding polish and sparkle to your sketch. The challenge with iridescent things is to show how they catch light and shift in color. That often means two or three colors in a tiny area (as on a button) so you need lots of fine-tip markers for this work.

USING PASTELS

PEARL
1. BABY PINK
2. BURGUNDY PENCIL
3. GEL PEN WHITE DOT

MOTHER-OF-PEARL
(PINK PENCIL,
LIME PENCIL)
1. DECO PINK
2. DECO ORANGE
3. PALE LIME

RHINESTONE (EXTRA PEN
LINE ACCENTS)
1. CLOUD BLUE
2. GRAY 30%
3. GRAY 60%

Four-Step Pearl Rendering

1. DOT OF MARKER COLOR
2. SEMIDOT IN WHITE GEL PEN ON TOP OF MARKER DOT
3. BLUE PENCIL HIGHLIGHT
4. DARK BLUE PENCIL (SHADOW SEMICIRCLE UNDER MARKER DOT)

TRIM LAYOUT

SHOE HIGHLIGHTS

COLORED TRIM ON SHOE'S PALE BACKGROUND

BOLDER OUTLINE FOR DARK BACKGROUND COLORS

Setup

For a white-on-white shoe or accessory, drop in your highlights accent color and plan where your trim will be placed.

Highlights and Shading

Special trims, like the pearls here, need to catch light and shadow to convey their roundness and make them look dimensional. It takes a lot of rendering in small spaces to make these decorative trims appealing and (somewhat) realistic. However stylized, you still want them to have a jewel-like quality in your sketch.

Darks

For a shoe or accessory with a dark background color behind the trim, start your rendering with that dark color. Outline your trim, so that it keeps its shape true to form. You're working in tight spaces so be patient and work slowly, keeping control over the color near all edges. Partial or loose rendering may not look luxe enough for these items.

Semiprecious Gems

Amber

1. Solid, flat base color
2. Blobs, bubbles, and dots of color accents
3. Tiny dots in darker colors
4. White gel pen gloss

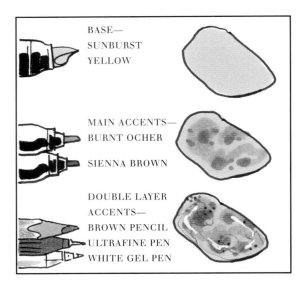

BASE—
SUNBURST
YELLOW

MAIN ACCENTS—
BURNT OCHER

SIENNA BROWN

DOUBLE LAYER
ACCENTS—
BROWN PENCIL
ULTRAFINE PEN
WHITE GEL PEN

Turquoise

1. Bits and dots of darker coloring
2. Base color surrounding but not over first layer of dots
3. Deeper background shadows
4. Hint of white gel pen sheen

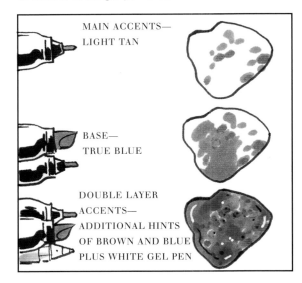

MAIN ACCENTS—
LIGHT TAN

BASE—
TRUE BLUE

DOUBLE LAYER
ACCENTS—
ADDITIONAL HINTS
OF BROWN AND BLUE
PLUS WHITE GEL PEN

Malachite

1. Solid, flat base color
2. Contoured, rounded color blobs
3. Darker color spirals all around contoured shape
4. White gel pen gleam

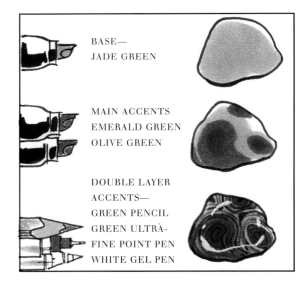

BASE—
JADE GREEN

MAIN ACCENTS
EMERALD GREEN
OLIVE GREEN

DOUBLE LAYER
ACCENTS—
GREEN PENCIL
GREEN ULTRA-
FINE POINT PEN
WHITE GEL PEN

Amethyst

1. Swirls of darker color
2. Matching swirls of lighter color leaving bits of white paper as accents
3. A hint of color pencil for reflected accent coloring
4. White gel pen sparkle

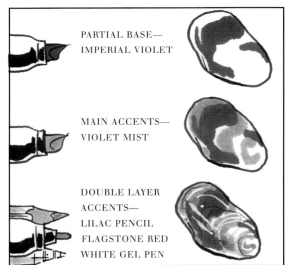

PARTIAL BASE—
IMPERIAL VIOLET

MAIN ACCENTS—
VIOLET MIST

DOUBLE LAYER
ACCENTS—
LILAC PENCIL
FLAGSTONE RED
WHITE GEL PEN

Metallics

Silver

Silver, pewter, chrome, platinum, and white gold can be rendered with metallic markers. Work from the lightest value into darker ones as accents.

BASE	GRAY 20%
MIDDLE VALUE	GRAY 30%
SHADOWS	GRAY 60%
SHINE	WHITE GEL PEN

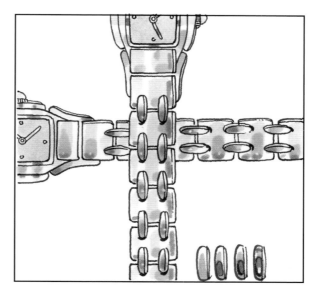

Gold

Gold, bronze, brass, and copper can be rendered with metallic or yellow and tan markers. Work from the brightest value to the deepest, leaving lots of "sparkle" highlights.

BASE	GOLDENROD
MIDDLE VALUE	BRONZE
SHADOWS	GOLD PENCIL
ACCENTS	BROWN FINE-POINT PEN
SHINE	WHITE GEL PEN

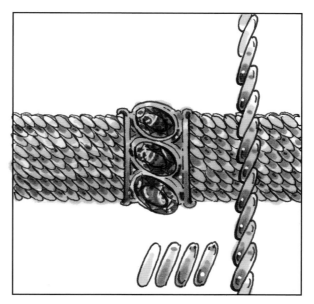

Semitransparent Fabrics

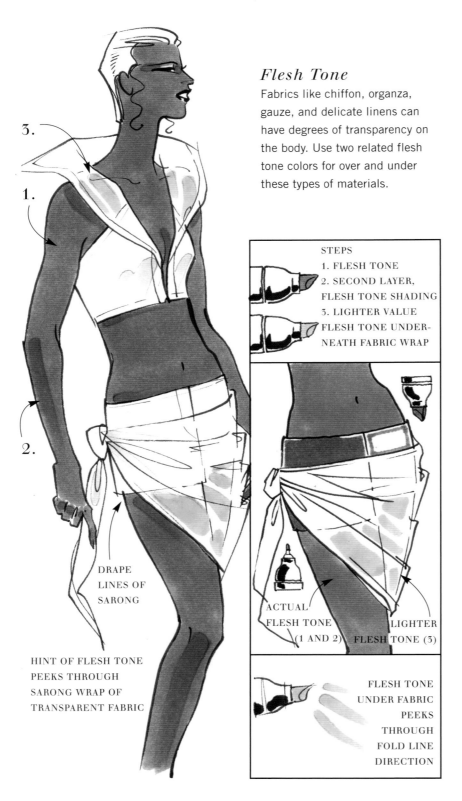

3.

1.

2.

DRAPE
LINES OF
SARONG

HINT OF FLESH TONE
PEEKS THROUGH
SARONG WRAP OF
TRANSPARENT FABRIC

Flesh Tone
Fabrics like chiffon, organza, gauze, and delicate linens can have degrees of transparency on the body. Use two related flesh tone colors for over and under these types of materials.

Transparent Fabric Layers
Fabrics with a see-through quality in solid colors or multicolor prints need two types of holding line— one for over the fabric and one for anything underneath it.

STEPS
1. FLESH TONE
2. SECOND LAYER,
   FLESH TONE SHADING
3. LIGHTER VALUE
   FLESH TONE UNDER-
   NEATH FABRIC WRAP

ACTUAL
FLESH TONE
(1 AND 2)   LIGHTER
          FLESH TONE (3)

FLESH TONE
UNDER FABRIC
PEEKS
THROUGH
FOLD LINE
DIRECTION

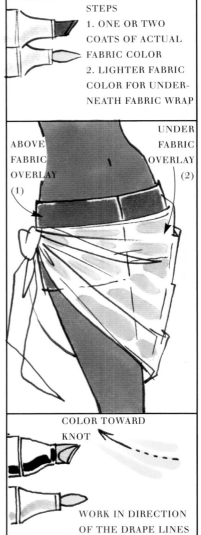

STEPS
1. ONE OR TWO
   COATS OF ACTUAL
   FABRIC COLOR
2. LIGHTER FABRIC
   COLOR FOR UNDER-
   NEATH FABRIC WRAP

ABOVE
FABRIC
OVERLAY
(1)

UNDER
FABRIC
OVERLAY
(2)

COLOR TOWARD
KNOT

WORK IN DIRECTION
OF THE DRAPE LINES

Print

Some prints are rendered on a white background. For these fabrics you can use the white of your paper as the print's base color. Apply the print over the other fabric rendering.

Texture

Often these types of fabrics have a grainy appearance because of their weave and their fiber. Use pencil over the marker to represent the grainy look of these materials.

Print and Texture

This combination of rendering requirements may seem like more work than is necessary. However, the extra work is worthwhile if the background or base color is different from the print color or if there is a mix of fabrics.

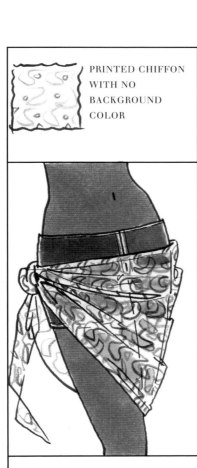

PRINTED CHIFFON WITH NO BACKGROUND COLOR

TWO-COLOR PRINT USING TWO COLORED PENCILS IN "POINT" METHOD

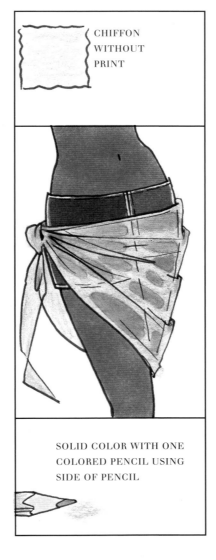

CHIFFON WITHOUT PRINT

SOLID COLOR WITH ONE COLORED PENCIL USING SIDE OF PENCIL

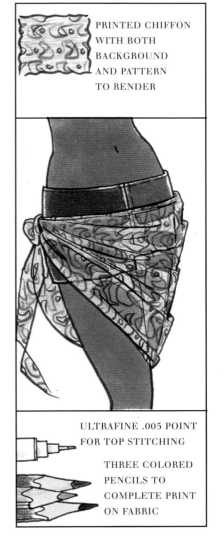

PRINTED CHIFFON WITH BOTH BACKGROUND AND PATTERN TO RENDER

ULTRAFINE .005 POINT FOR TOP STITCHING

THREE COLORED PENCILS TO COMPLETE PRINT ON FABRIC

Monochromatic Color Schemes

COORDINATED
FABRIC MIXES

BLENDING
COLOR
LAYERS

FABRIC
MIXES

BARK   BURNT OCHER   DARK UMBER

MONOCHROMATIC
COLORS

RENDERING
VARIETY
FOR MONOCHROMATIC
COLOR SCHEMES

Coordinated, monochromatic color schemes in fabric mixes call for multiple rendering techniques in order to accentuate the subtle or pronounced differences between types of material. For example, you could render a brushed suede next to an embossed leather over a knit paired with a wool gabardine. The trick is to accomplish all that rendering variety with as many shortcuts or time-saving methods as possible.

SUPPLIES:
3 MARKERS
1 PENCIL
1 PEN

KNIT
SWATCHES

RIBS   ROWS   SEED STITCHES

BRAID   CHAIN   CABLE

CASHMERE   MOHAIR OR   BOUCLÉ
             ANGORA

HEATHERED
YARNS

Knits can be slightly easier than wovens to render in a monochromatic color scheme because the variety of their stitch and yarn pattern leaves you with lots of sketching options. For all the fabrics, knits, and wovens, here and on page 154, it only took three markers, one pen, and one pencil to render. The techniques illustrated here would work in any color on any design concept in fashion, accessories, or home fashion.

Dark Color Prints

Plaids are introduced as prints on a grid in Chapter 5. The plaid on this page is more dense and therefore requires more steps and more colors. It starts off as a kind of gingham over a solid background color and then builds up into five colors in six steps. Any more work than this on a small sketch gets diminishing returns because of the time invested. A good rule of thumb to follow is don't overrender if possible.

For all layers that build a plaid, use pen or pencil last for the thinnest lines in the print motif. This is also a good idea because fine lines can be smeared when you use a broad nib marker over them.

Plaid Rendering Stages

FIRST LAYER: BASE COLOR— SAND

SECOND LAYER: BROADEST GRID— BURNT OCHER

THIRD LAYER: GRID CENTERS— GRAY 60%

FOURTH LAYER: SMALLER, THINNER GRID

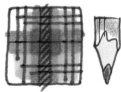

FIFTH LAYER: DIAGONAL LINE GRID— DARK BROWN PENCIL

RENDERING OF THIRD LAYER RESEMBLES A COMPLETED GINGHAM PRINT

SIXTH LAYER: PEN POINT CENTERS ON THIN GRID LINES

COMPLETE GRID CENTERS WITH BLACK DOTS AT CROSSOVER PRINTS

PLAID FINISHED

PLAID IN PROGRESS

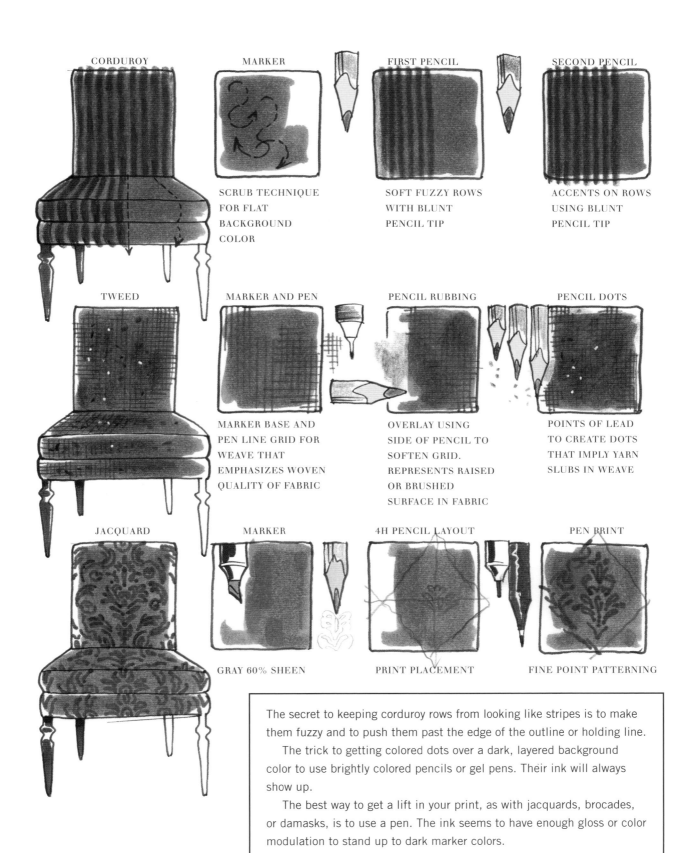

CORDUROY

MARKER

SCRUB TECHNIQUE
FOR FLAT
BACKGROUND
COLOR

FIRST PENCIL

SOFT FUZZY ROWS
WITH BLUNT
PENCIL TIP

SECOND PENCIL

ACCENTS ON ROWS
USING BLUNT
PENCIL TIP

TWEED

MARKER AND PEN

MARKER BASE AND
PEN LINE GRID FOR
WEAVE THAT
EMPHASIZES WOVEN
QUALITY OF FABRIC

PENCIL RUBBING

OVERLAY USING
SIDE OF PENCIL TO
SOFTEN GRID.
REPRESENTS RAISED
OR BRUSHED
SURFACE IN FABRIC

PENCIL DOTS

POINTS OF LEAD
TO CREATE DOTS
THAT IMPLY YARN
SLUBS IN WEAVE

JACQUARD

MARKER

GRAY 60% SHEEN

4H PENCIL LAYOUT

PRINT PLACEMENT

PEN PRINT

FINE POINT PATTERNING

The secret to keeping corduroy rows from looking like stripes is to make
them fuzzy and to push them past the edge of the outline or holding line.

The trick to getting colored dots over a dark, layered background
color to use brightly colored pencils or gel pens. Their ink will always
show up.

The best way to get a lift in your print, as with jacquards, brocades,
or damasks, is to use a pen. The ink seems to have enough gloss or color
modulation to stand up to dark marker colors.

Rendering Leathers

Leathers and suedes come in all sorts of mock or authentic finishes including matte, shiny, smooth, and rough, with all kinds of looks and materials as well. Many leather designs come with lots of trims and notions—zippers, grommets, snaps, and top stitching. Start with the basics in color, surface, and texture before you try to handle all the complexities of design details. Dark colors are a good place to start for leathers and suedes. Deep colors, especially for menswear, are the most common. The examples here focus on layered color, shading, and highlights.

One- and Two-Step Methods

MATTE LEATHER, QUICK METHOD: NO SHADOWS. HIGHLIGHTS ONLY.   1. BASE COAT: ULTRAMARINE   2. SHADING/DETAILS: NAVY BLUE WITH WHITE LINE

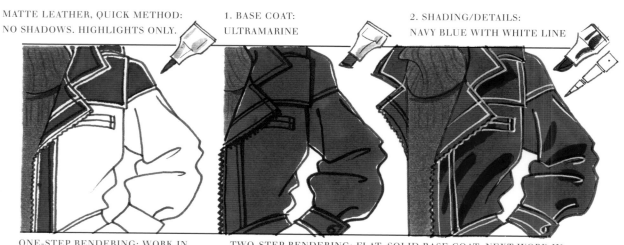

ONE-STEP RENDERING: WORK IN COLOR SECTIONS. COLOR UP TO BUT NOT TOUCHING OUTLINE AND SEAM.

TWO-STEP RENDERING: FLAT, SOLID BASE COAT. NEXT WORK IN SHADOWS. REOUTLINE IN WHITE GEL PEN.

SHINY LEATHER, QUICK METHOD: NO SHADOWS. HIGHLIGHTS ONLY.   1. BASE COAT: GRAY 70%   2. SHADING/DETAILS: BLACK WITH WHITE LINE

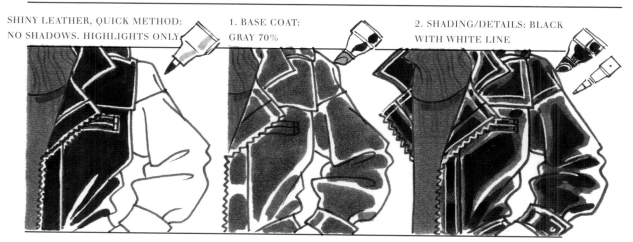

ONE-STEP RENDERING: WORK IN SMALL UNITS. COLOR UP TO BUT NOT OVER THE OUTLINE.

TWO-STEP RENDERING: START WITH SECTIONS IN GRAY. LEAVE WHITE FROM PAPER AS MAJOR HIGHLIGHTS. WORK BLACK OVER (ON TOP OF) THE GRAY IN MATCHING BUT SMALL SECTIONS. REOUTLINE IN WHITE GEL PEN.

Three-Step Method

1. BASE   2. SHADING   3. BRUSHED SURFACE

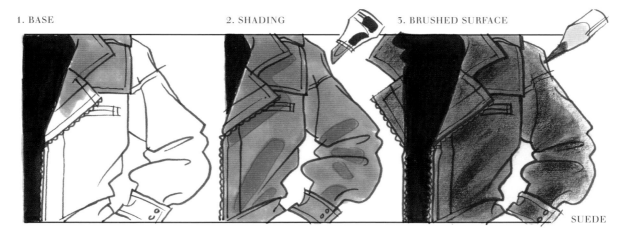

SUEDE

Start rendering suede in the same steps as for matte leathers—solid base coat with shadows. Use the shadows to accentuate details, cut, or layers in the design shape. Add colored pencil for the sueded brushed surface.

EMBOSSED LEATHER

Begin rendering embossed or printed leather with a solid base color. For darker colors, like browns or navies, you need up to three values of one color for luster without shine. The lightest value is the base color. The middle value is the second layer. The deepest value is the last step before defining the print with a colored pencil or pen line.

HEAVYWEIGHT LEATHER

Heavyweight leathers get deeper coloring to convey their thickness. In monochromatic coloring schemes the deepest and last layer is the emphasized color value. It is rendered leaving just enough of the lighter value colors so that detail is not obliterated. Here the coloring method gives the leather less luster but more volume.

Dark Color Weaves

Deep colors such as navy blue are a challenge because, done badly, they appear stiff or wooden and obliterate design detail. The solution is to illustrate the reflective quality of light and dark in a fabric. This tonality softens the dark colors and solves the problem of the outline being obliterated by the dark color. With this method your first color layer is the true color of the fabric. After the second layer is added, you can introduce any weave, texture, or print that has to go over the navy blue, burgundy, or other dark colored materials. To make the surface details show up, you'll need to use either black or white pens or pencils for contrast.

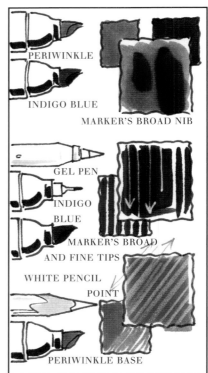

PERIWINKLE

INDIGO BLUE

MARKER'S BROAD NIB

GEL PEN

INDIGO BLUE

MARKER'S BROAD AND FINE TIPS

WHITE PENCIL POINT

PERIWINKLE BASE

Navy Blue Trousers

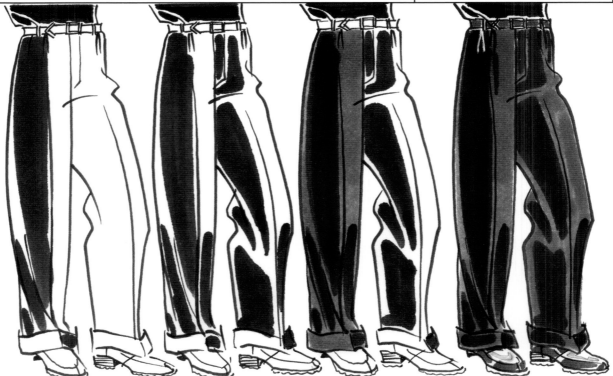

DARKER COLOR USED FIRST, WITH PARTIAL OR LOOSE RENDERING TO CREATE HIGHTLIGHTS.

LIGHTER COLOR USED LAST ON TOP OF OR NEXT TO THE DARKER COLOR. RENDER AS IF TO CREATE A SOLID BASE COLOR WITH SHADOWS.

Alternate Weaves and Patterns for Same Base Color

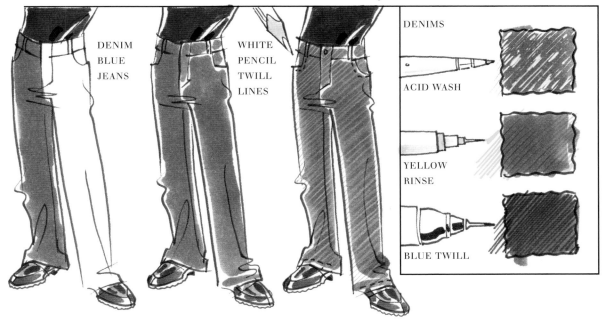

DENIM BLUE JEANS

WHITE PENCIL TWILL LINES

DENIMS

ACID WASH

YELLOW RINSE

BLUE TWILL

Here is where you get to practice all sorts of pen line and pencil methods over a two-step marker rendering technique. The results will be as varied as all the examples here, plus new ones you now have the skills to invent.

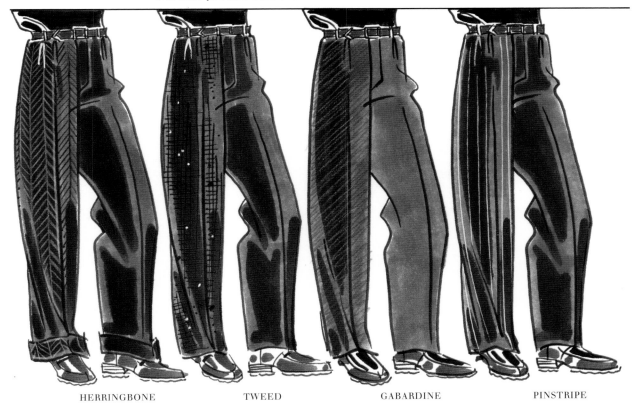

HERRINGBONE   TWEED   GABARDINE   PINSTRIPE

Using the same base color you can render fabrics from light blue chambray to dark blue denims.

Mixing Light and Dark Fabrics

THREE-MARKER RENDERING, ANY BRAND,
ANY ANALOGOUS COLORS, SAME RESULTS

LIGHTEST VALUE FIRST —
DARKEST VALUE LAST

SIMPLE VERSION:
CHIFFON OVER
SOLID FABRIC

PENCIL FOR
DOTTED SWISS
CHIFFON FOR CONTRAST

THREE-COLOR BASE
FOR MOSAIC PRINT
GEL PEN GRID FOR
FINISH ON MOSAIC
PRINT

SOLID MATTE COLOR—
LEAVE ALL SEAM LINES
UNCOLORED SO CONSTRUCTION
OR CUT IS NOT OBLITERATED

SILKY SOLID COLOR FABRIC—
LAYERING FROM LIGHT TO
DARK IN SIMILAR INCREMENTS

SOME
OF THE GRID PEEKS
THROUGH THE CHIFFON
DRAPE OVER THE CHAIR

STEP 1.
PRINT PLAN

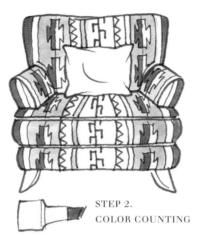

STEP 2.
COLOR COUNTING

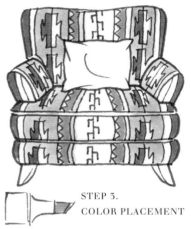

STEP 3.
COLOR PLACEMENT

Multicolor Prints

Even with abbreviating a print's motif and reducing the actual number of its colors, some fabrics still need extra steps—more planning and color counting. Save the darkest colors and weave impressions for last.

Dark Solid Colors

To save time and having to return all your outline cuts and seams, keep the color away from edges and seams as you apply the marker. Work in sections, coloring one part at a time, instead of coloring in the shape and losing detail.

Fabric Mixes

The options are to work at completing one fabric at a time or one color at a time, or to finish all marker rendering before using pen or vice versa. Just remember that marker does not go over pencil well. Save colored pen line and gel pen details for last because marker could make those inks run or disappear.

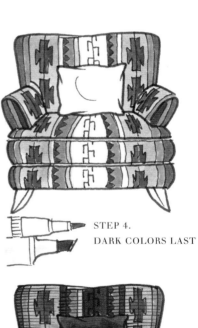

STEP 4.
DARK COLORS LAST

STEP 5.
FINE-LINE PEN
FOR WEAVE

Glass and Pottery

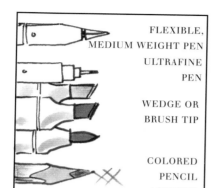

FLEXIBLE,
MEDIUM WEIGHT PEN

ULTRAFINE
PEN

WEDGE OR
BRUSH TIP

COLORED
PENCIL
ACCENTS

Glass

Glass is so reflective that it catches light influences from all the colors near it. If you are rendering glass by itself, then you have to decide if it's going to get cool or warm tones. Cool tones with frosted blues are demonstrated here. The challenge is to get your line as delicate as your coloring.

SOFT LINES / CUT GLASS

HARD LINES / FLUTED POTTERY

GLASS

POTTERY

Pottery

Pottery is done in many media and can range from grainy like clay to polished like glass. In contrast to glass, which gets lots of highlights, pottery can be rendered with just a line of "shimmer." Its coloring can get lots of tonality, appearing solid, especially if it is glazed as illustrated here.

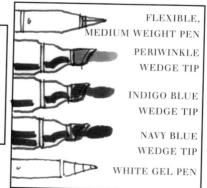

FLEXIBLE,
MEDIUM WEIGHT PEN

PERIWINKLE
WEDGE TIP

INDIGO BLUE
WEDGE TIP

NAVY BLUE
WEDGE TIP

WHITE GEL PEN

FROM GLASS
TO CUT GLASS
TO ETCHED GLASS

ONE FLAT
BASE LAYER

THREE-LAYER
SHADOWS

TWO-LAYER
HIGHLIGHTS

 WEDGE NIB—
OVERALL CRISP,
SHARP COLORING

 BRUSH TIP—
EXPRESSIVE,
SPONTANEOUS
COLORING

 FINE POINT—
THIN, PRECISION
COLORING

 COLORED PENCIL—
SOFT LINE DETAILING

 WHITE GEL PEN OR PAINT—
HIGH, GLOSSY SHIMMER

Glass can be rendered to catch more light than shadows. Pottery can get both light and shadow. Shading for pottery adds to its volume, while the light gives it polish. Together they accentuate the form and contours of pottery pieces.

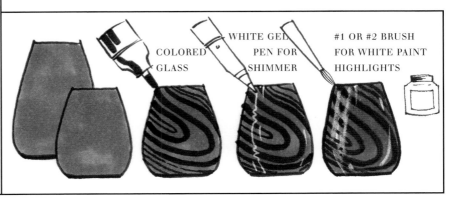

COLORED
GLASS

WHITE GEL
PEN FOR
SHIMMER

#1 OR #2 BRUSH
FOR WHITE PAINT
HIGHLIGHTS

Accessories in Black

Gloves On or off the hands, gloves look quite natural with a highlight across the knuckles. This keeps them from looking stiff or wooden, and softens the solid black rendering.

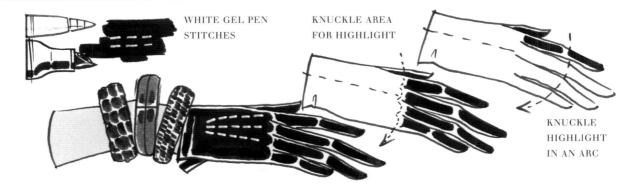

WHITE GEL PEN
STITCHES

KNUCKLE AREA
FOR HIGHLIGHT

KNUCKLE
HIGHLIGHT
IN AN ARC

Wallets These items can get a smooth black like gloves. But when it comes to textures you want to bulk up the outline contour, from smooth to textured. Here are two methods for creating the look of skins or embossed leathers.

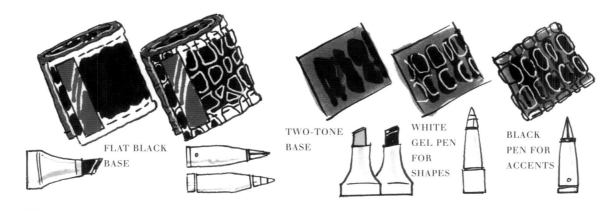

FLAT BLACK
BASE

TWO-TONE
BASE

WHITE
GEL PEN
FOR
SHAPES

BLACK
PEN FOR
ACCENTS

Bags This is where trims and notions become the focal point for rendering. Accents or embellishments on straps, for instance, remind you of how critical line quality and variety are to the success of your sketch.

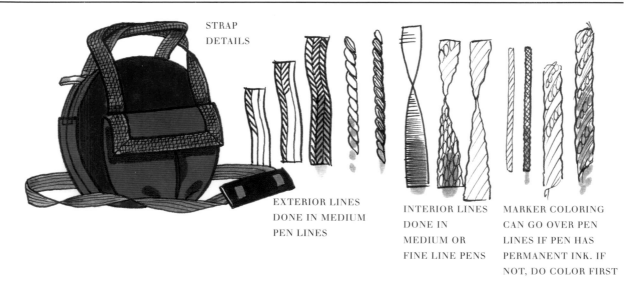

STRAP
DETAILS

EXTERIOR LINES
DONE IN MEDIUM
PEN LINES

INTERIOR LINES
DONE IN
MEDIUM OR
FINE LINE PENS

MARKER COLORING
CAN GO OVER PEN
LINES IF PEN HAS
PERMANENT INK. IF
NOT, DO COLOR FIRST

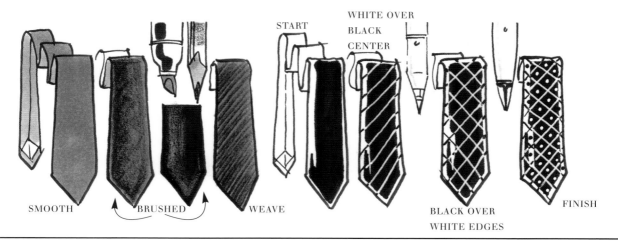

Ties Whether you start in gray layers to create a black fabric or go directly into black, you need to incorporate pen and pencil techniques to complete most prints.

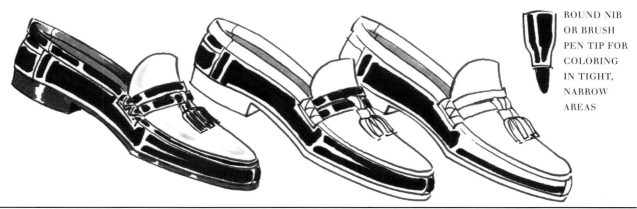

Shoes Glossy black patent leather or high-shine looks come with sleek, narrow highlights that accentuate the shape as well as the material of the shoe.

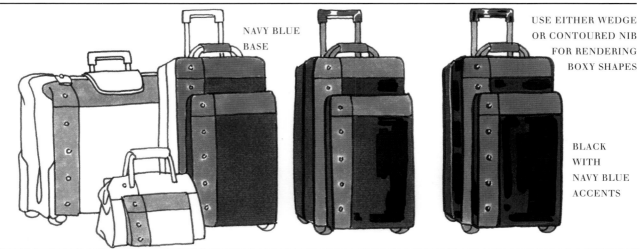

Luggage It makes sense to give black fabrics dark color accents or highlights to soften the silhouette and keep the details evident. Matte fabrics don't have reflective qualities, but you need to add some reflection to liven up the solid flat coloring.

Glamour Fabrics in Black

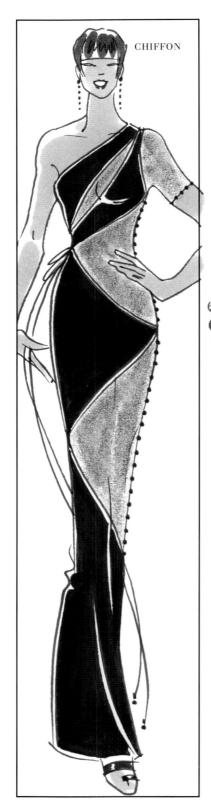

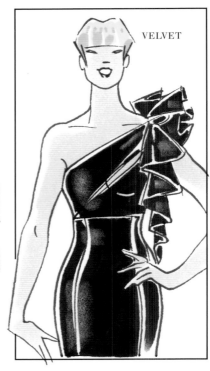

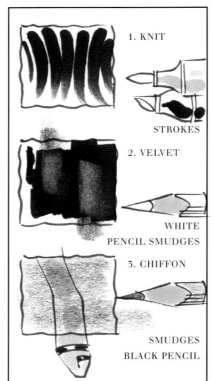

All these fabrics are covered in preceding chapters, but they look intimidating when rendering in black. Most use the same four supplies to complete.

1. **Knits:** Easiest method is to use color strokes to signify knit rows or ribbing.
2. **Velvet:** White pencil smudging. No color by the seams.
3. **Chiffon:** Render the marker first. Add pencil smudging next.

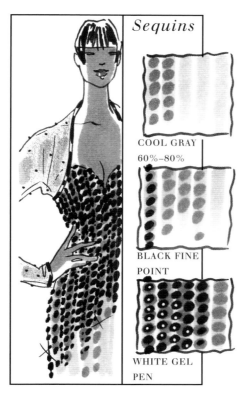

Sequins

COOL GRAY 60%–80%

BLACK FINE POINT

WHITE GEL PEN

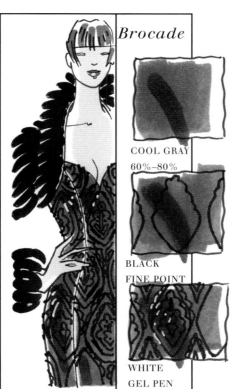

Brocade

COOL GRAY 60%–80%

BLACK FINE POINT

WHITE GEL PEN

Sequins

To suggest iridescence, use two or three layers of grays to give the impression of color modulation. Use white gel pen for a bit of sparkle.

Lace

Before doing cross-hatching for the delicate weave, add the marker flesh tone or fabric color beneath the lace first.

Jacquard

This fabric gets light and shadow. The print over the background color flips from black over the highlights to white over the shading.

Brocade

This raised print is done with the same method as the one used for jacquard, but it uses fewer highlights. Work in the deepest gray values with true black as the shadows so that the black print can be seen.

Taffeta

If this crisp fabric is not shiny you can actually highlight it in a deep gray to suggest a bit of glass in the fabric. (The jacket is taffeta; the dress is velvet.)

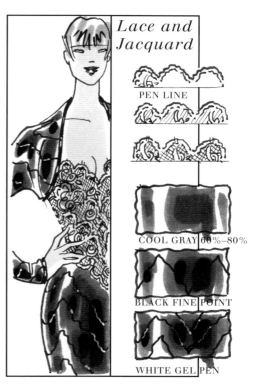

Lace and Jacquard

PEN LINE

COOL GRAY 60%–80%

BLACK FINE POINT

WHITE GEL PEN

Taffeta

COOL GRAY: 70%

BLACK CONTOURED NIB

PENCIL

Assignment

Between the light and dark coloring methods, metallics, and complex print techniques, you have a lot of rendering options to use in an assignment. Be gutsy and look for a challenging print to do. Why? Because once you've done a difficult fabric, such fabrics can't intimidate you anymore.

Select a shape to render from either the fashion, accessories, or home decor category. Draw the shape three times in a row on a page.

The first sketch is for the print's layout. Plan its repeats on the first shape.

On the second shape you have to color count; that is, you have to figure out how many colors to use and in what order they go on the sketch.

Now you are ready to render. You understand the print. The colors are lined up and ready to go.

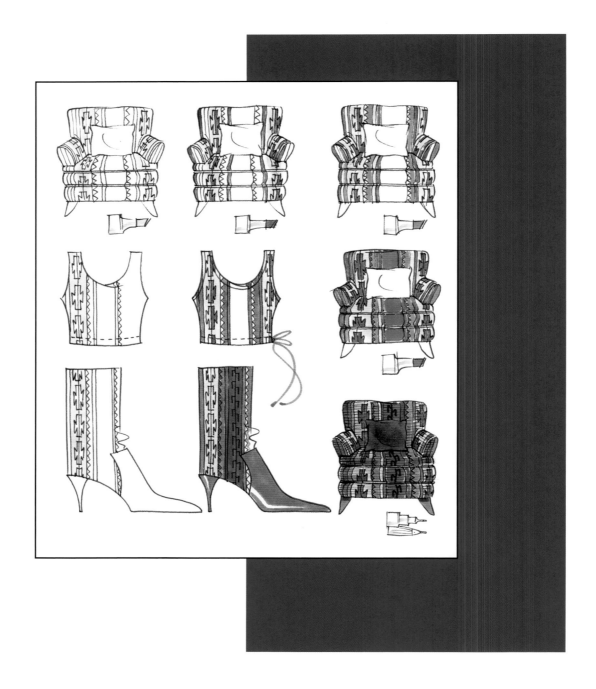

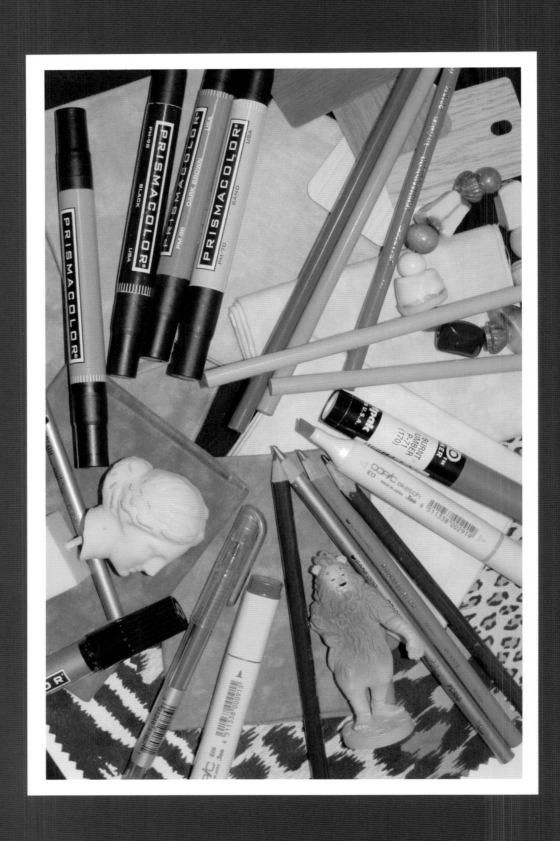

TEXTURES

Checklist

Markers   By exploring rendering techniques for textures, you can expand your creativity. You need to get the most into and out of a small, 9-inch by 12-inch or 11-inch by 14-inch sketch. You also need to work with the time constraints that deadlines present.

Learn to work quickly and efficiently by testing the range of your media and your imagination. You have to learn how to manipulate the way in which you hold and move your markers, pencils, and pens to master their potential.

You need to do test strips to familiarize yourself with the potential for pressure and release in marker line and coloring. It's important to invent new techniques for your own style by knowing what the old ones are.

Creating test strips is the equivalent of a musician playing the scales to warm up before a performance. It loosens you up and fine-tunes your senses. Your media are your instrument.

Pencils   Textured surfaces have many complexities and present an interesting challenge when rendering with pencil. Focus on both interior and exterior line quality when using this medium. To master the lessons presented in this chapter, you must become flexible enough with the pencil to render fuzzy, subtle textures differently than wild, bold textures. That takes practice and imagination.

Pens   Pens are a vital tool in rendering layers in textures. You must remember that pens have a penchant for extra ink blobbing up—too much ink—or for the pen drying out—too little ink. These are problems we all encounter. To protect your sketch, keep a test strip next to your art page to practice your line before you use a pen on your real sketch.

Test Page

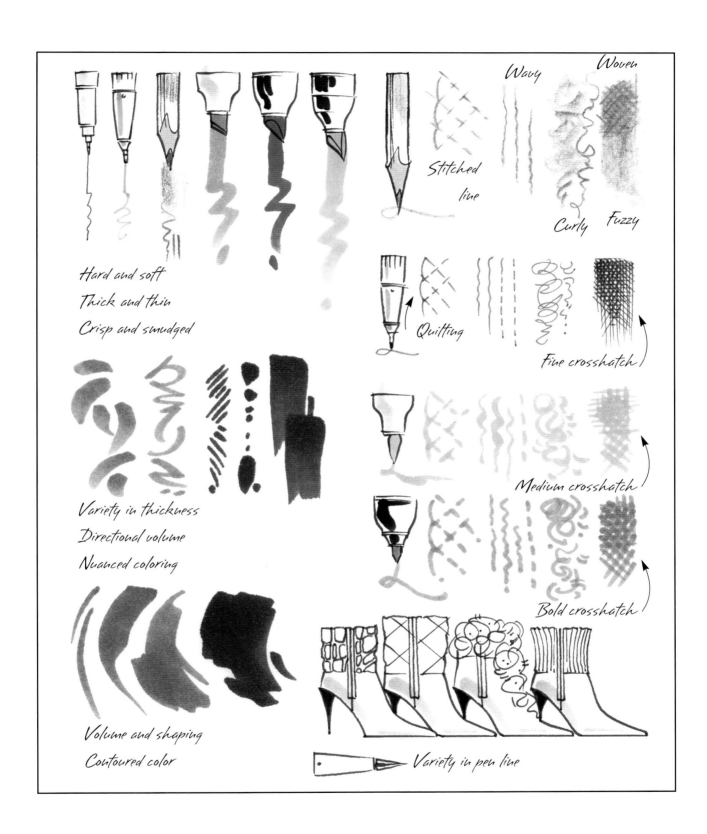

Hard and soft
Thick and thin
Crisp and smudged

Variety in thickness
Directional volume
Nuanced coloring

Volume and shaping
Contoured color

Wavy

Woven

Stitched line

Curly

Fuzzy

Quilting

Fine crosshatch

Medium crosshatch

Bold crosshatch

Variety in pen line

Rattan, Wicker, and Natural Fibers

Rattan and wicker come in many varieties of woven patterns. They can be painted in a host of colors but are most often in their natural earth tone browns. After weave and color selection, the rendering process is usually divided between the bolder, heavier look of the rattan chair (below) and the finer, more delicate appearance of the wicker basket (right). Brush tips or flexible contoured marker nibs are great for thicker rattan. Ultrafine pens or the thin tip of a marker are best for wicker basket reedlike weaves. Colored pencils are an asset in developing complex weave patterns, creating surface interest, and accentuating color nuances.

Wicker Baskets

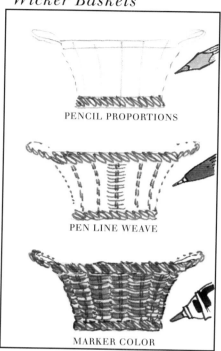

PENCIL PROPORTIONS

PEN LINE WEAVE

MARKER COLOR

Rattan and Wicker

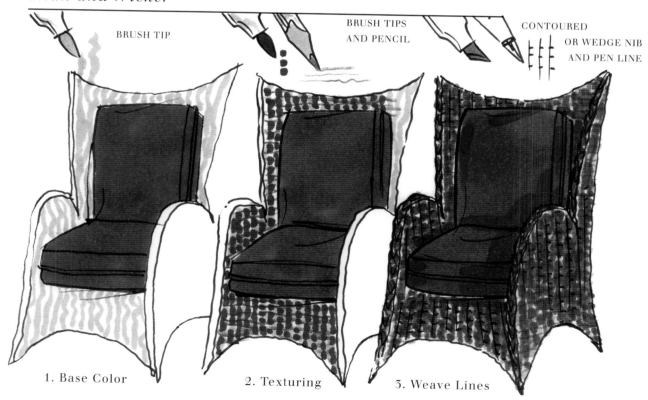

BRUSH TIP

BRUSH TIPS AND PENCIL

CONTOURED OR WEDGE NIB AND PEN LINE

1. Base Color

2. Texturing

3. Weave Lines

Bamboo — One of Many Patterns

1. Completed rows, light
2. Intermittent rows, dark
3. Pencil thread lines

The look—slick, linear, flat

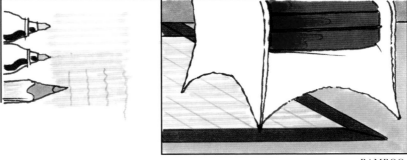

BAMBOO

Jute — One of Many Patterns

1. Solid background
2. Basket weave setup
3. Pencil "hits" to raise weave

The look—textural, rough, coarse

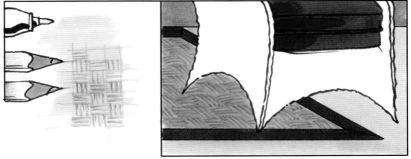

JUTE

Sisal — One of Many Patterns

1. Irregular rows of uneven weight
2. Color slubs dot across the rows
3. Pencil weave lines

The look—tight, rigid, ribbed

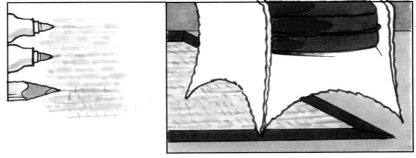

SISAL

Mountain Grass — One of Many Patterns

1. Herringbone weave lines
2. Uneven dashes in between weave lines
3. Pencil lines to add texture

The look—dimensional, rough, thick

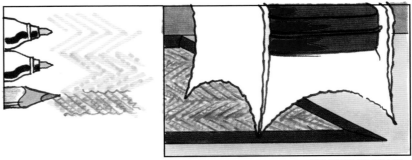

MOUNTAIN GRASS

Wood and Masonry

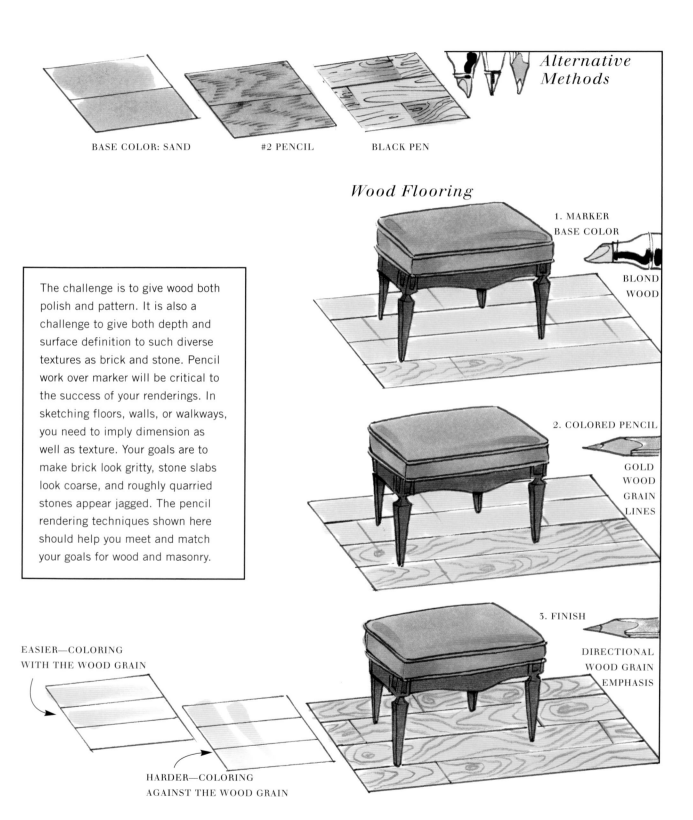

BASE COLOR: SAND

#2 PENCIL

BLACK PEN

Alternative Methods

Wood Flooring

The challenge is to give wood both polish and pattern. It is also a challenge to give both depth and surface definition to such diverse textures as brick and stone. Pencil work over marker will be critical to the success of your renderings. In sketching floors, walls, or walkways, you need to imply dimension as well as texture. Your goals are to make brick look gritty, stone slabs look coarse, and roughly quarried stones appear jagged. The pencil rendering techniques shown here should help you meet and match your goals for wood and masonry.

1. MARKER BASE COLOR

BLOND WOOD

2. COLORED PENCIL

GOLD WOOD GRAIN LINES

3. FINISH

DIRECTIONAL WOOD GRAIN EMPHASIS

EASIER—COLORING WITH THE WOOD GRAIN

HARDER—COLORING AGAINST THE WOOD GRAIN

Consider these three rendering techniques from gritty to coarse to jagged as the basis for all the rest of the varieties in brick and stonework. Colors and uses for these materials may change, but the marker and pencil work will be relatively the same.

Brickwork: Gritty

THREE- TO
FOUR-COLOR
MIX

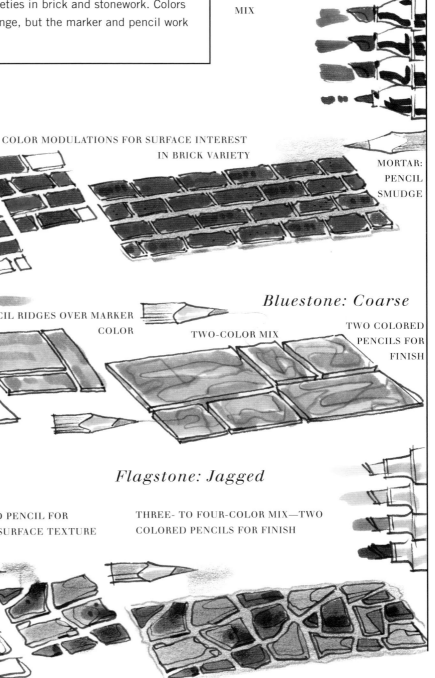

MORTAR:
PENCIL
SMUDGE

LAYOUT: GET ANGLED
EDGES FOR BRICK OUTLINE

COLOR MODULATIONS FOR SURFACE INTEREST
IN BRICK VARIETY

ANGULAR COLOR
BLOCKING

PENCIL RIDGES OVER MARKER
COLOR

Bluestone: Coarse

TWO-COLOR MIX

TWO COLORED
PENCILS FOR
FINISH

Flagstone: Jagged

COLOR MODULATIONS
FOR IRREGULAR STONE
SURFACES AND CUTS

COLORED PENCIL FOR
JAGGED SURFACE TEXTURE

THREE- TO FOUR-COLOR MIX—TWO
COLORED PENCILS FOR FINISH

COLOR AND TEXTURE FOR ANY
MEDIUM LIKE MORTAR BETWEEN
STONEWORK CAN VARY

Exaggerating Texture

Exaggeration in detail can emphasize color, weave, or print. It can also build contrast between surfaces such as those that may be smooth or textured. This exaggeration plays up the design features, and gets the image strong. Overstatement as dramatic license means making sure that between your outline edging and interior coloring you have maximized the potential in contrasts, especially for textures.

Collar

Exaggerate the volume and cut in design of the collar by pumping up curl in the fibers.

Rug

Emphasize the depth of the pile in the rug by having the furniture sink into the rug.

Coverlet

Establish the contrast between fabrics in your sketch by maximizing the differences between exterior and interior lines and textures.

Trim

Embolden nuances in style by making the surface textures more dramatic in outline and in color.

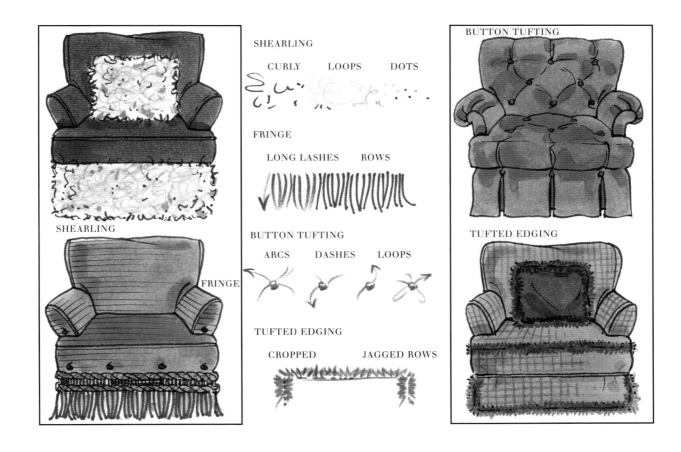

SHEARLING

CURLY   LOOPS   DOTS

FRINGE

LONG LASHES   ROWS

BUTTON TUFTING

ARCS   DASHES   LOOPS

TUFTED EDGING

CROPPED   JAGGED ROWS

SHEARLING

FRINGE

BUTTON TUFTING

TUFTED EDGING

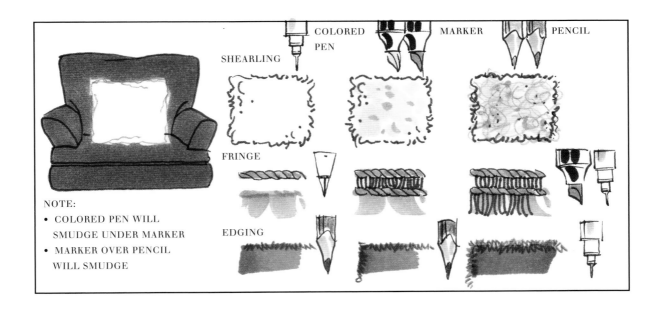

COLORED PEN   MARKER   PENCIL

SHEARLING

FRINGE

EDGING

NOTE:
• COLORED PEN WILL
  SMUDGE UNDER MARKER
• MARKER OVER PENCIL
  WILL SMUDGE

Furs

Fake furs can look as real as the authentic furs. The textile industry has an amazing array of mock and faux everything, all of which is luxe to look at and illustrate.

Short hair fibers like mink need a smooth brushed surface appearance. Medium to long fibers like fox need directional lines and color. Extra long fibers like bear are shaggy and heavy looking. Tightly rolled and curly hair, like Persian lamb, needs wavy, loopy lines and color.

An integral part of rendering fur is illustrating the outline edge. It can be done with pen, colored pen, or colored pencil as long as the line is clear and crisp.

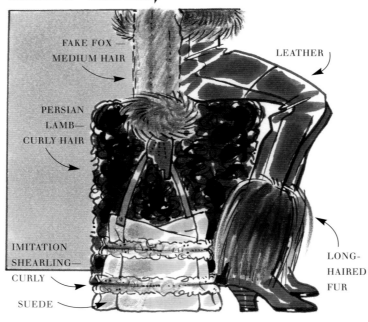

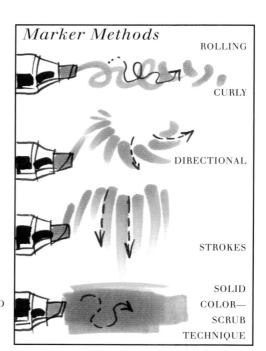

SHORT
FUR

MEDIUM
FUR

LONG
FUR

CURLY
FUR

Animal Prints

Although animal prints can be dyed to match fashion trends, the authentic coloring for these wild prints can vary according to personal preferences. Tiger can be more yellow orange, leopard can be paler or darker, giraffe might be darker with larger spots, and so on.

This page and the page opposite provide information for making each print look different from another. Your rendering goal should be to make the prints instantly recognizable. Notice that to make these prints look like fur, you can add some pencil "fiber" lines over the marker coloring (as on page 187).

Animal prints are often used in non-traditional ways, such as a leopard-spot pattern woven into denim, or a zebra print on a delicate handkerchief. These examples demonstrate that sometimes a print's motif is more important than its color.

TIGER

LEOPARD

ZEBRA

GIRAFFE

DALMATION

PONY

TIGER

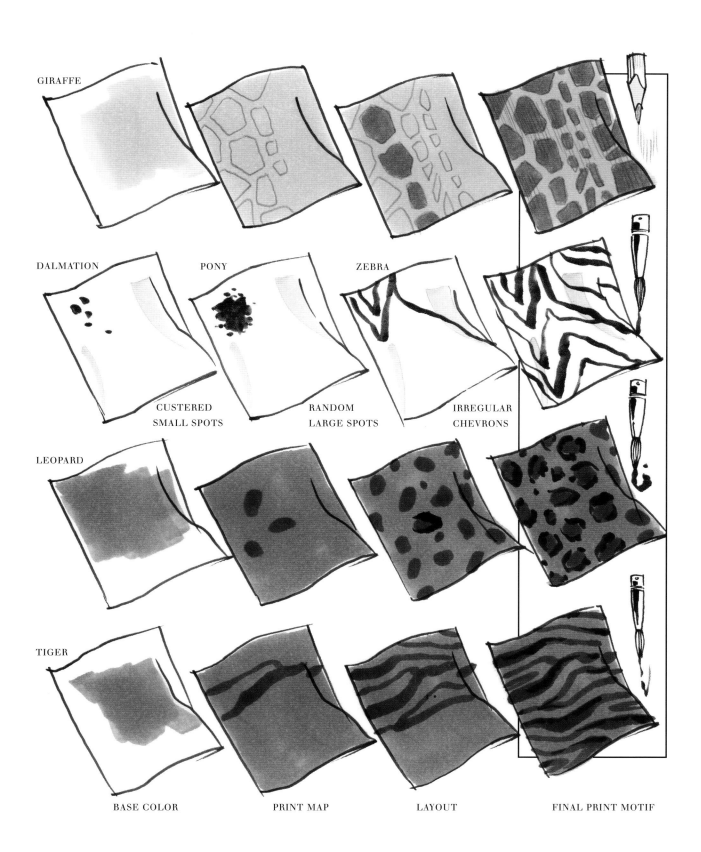

GIRAFFE

DALMATION   PONY   ZEBRA

CUSTERED   RANDOM   IRREGULAR
SMALL SPOTS   LARGE SPOTS   CHEVRONS

LEOPARD

TIGER

BASE COLOR   PRINT MAP   LAYOUT   FINAL PRINT MOTIF

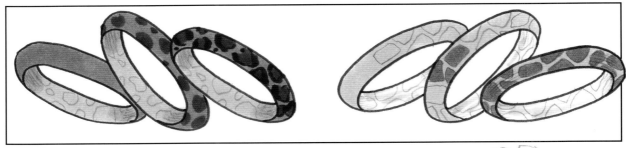

#4H PENCIL, IRREGULAR SPOTS

#4H PENCIL, SHAPED AND SPACED SPOTS

BRUSH PEN, SQUIGGLY LINES

BRUSH PEN, IRREGULARLY SPACED STRIPES

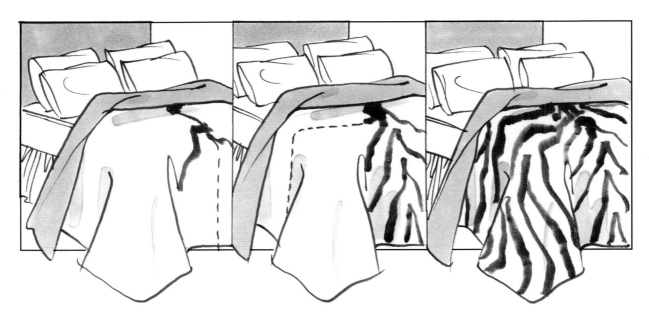

Accessories

Black and white animal printed shapes need some gray shading to help to define contours and suggest dimension.

BRUSH PEN SPOTS

GRAY 30% FOR INSIDE CURVE IN BRACELET

BRUSH PEN SPOTS AND STRIPING

Fashion

Fashion animal prints can be done with or without the furry outline edges. You have the option of rendering them smooth or furry.

BRUSH PEN SPOTS
PENCIL LINE AND SMUDGING

COLORED PENCIL FOR LIFT ON FUR

FINE BRUSH PEN FOR EMPHASIZING EDGES

Home Fashions

You need to practice adding other elements to the animal prints such as quilted fabric or any other stitch treatments that will add to your rendering skills.

PEN LINE FOR QUILTING
STITCHES

Skins

Before you get into the natural looks for embossed leathers, mock crocodile, and other skins, study some of the rendering techniques that are related to these textures. Notice how important outline edges are to these looks. Think about what skills you have already learned that can be adapted to these new textures.

Some of the line variety that you learned in Chapter 1 becomes an integral part in creating believable images for skins, embossed leathers, and the other raised surfaces illustrated in this spread. Exaggerated outline definition always adds an extra visual interest to your sketches.

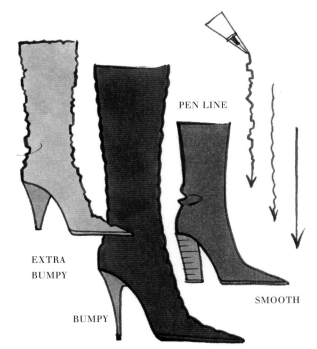

PEN LINE

EXTRA
BUMPY

BUMPY

SMOOTH

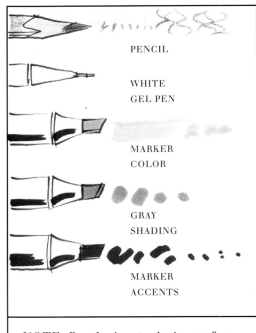

PENCIL

WHITE
GEL PEN

MARKER
COLOR

GRAY
SHADING

MARKER
ACCENTS

NOTE: Rendering techniques for stitching (features like quilting) overlap with mock crocodile and other skin rendering methods.

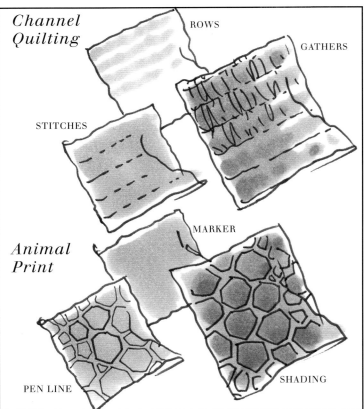

Channel Quilting

ROWS

GATHERS

STITCHES

MARKER

Animal Print

PEN LINE

SHADING

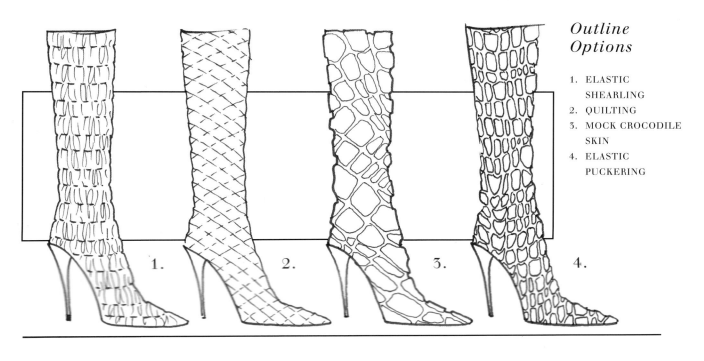

Outline Options

1. ELASTIC SHEARLING
2. QUILTING
3. MOCK CROCODILE SKIN
4. ELASTIC PUCKERING

1.
2.
3.
4.

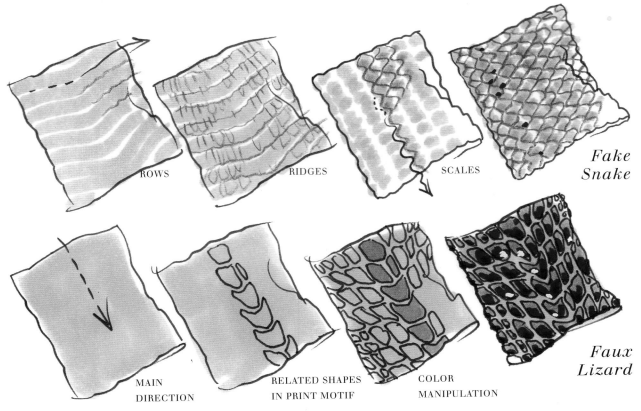

ROWS

RIDGES

SCALES

Fake Snake

MAIN DIRECTION

RELATED SHAPES IN PRINT MOTIF

COLOR MANIPULATION

Faux Lizard

Skin Prints

With or without authentic coloring for these skin looks, you can still tell that each is different from the other in these examples. So it is not as much about color as it is about the patterning of each separate skin type. Your rendering skills will make each look unique and accurate, without being labor-intensive. Your rendering goal is to be able to do these quickly and make them look compelling.

Trims and notions, such as belt buckles, can be just as challenging to render as any texture or print. This is an opportunity to practice drawing the smooth surface of metal, the knobby contours of bamboo, and the scrunched fibers of hemp.

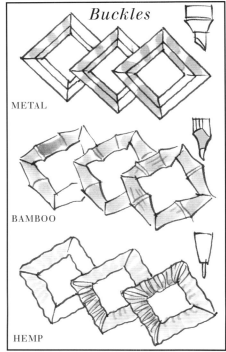

Buckles

METAL

BAMBOO

HEMP

COLORED PEN
COLORED PENCIL

MARKER

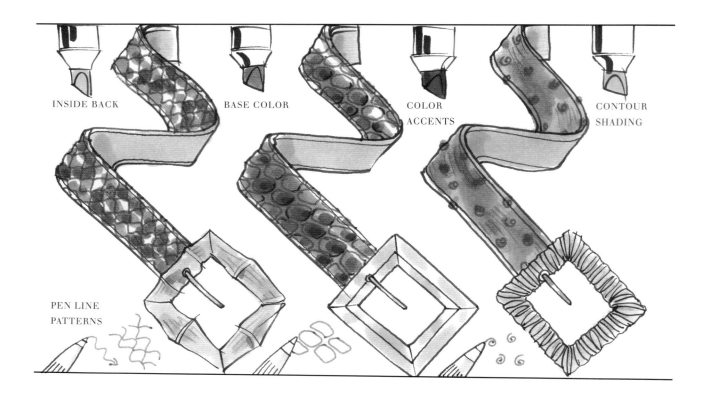

INSIDE BACK

BASE COLOR

COLOR ACCENTS

CONTOUR SHADING

PEN LINE PATTERNS

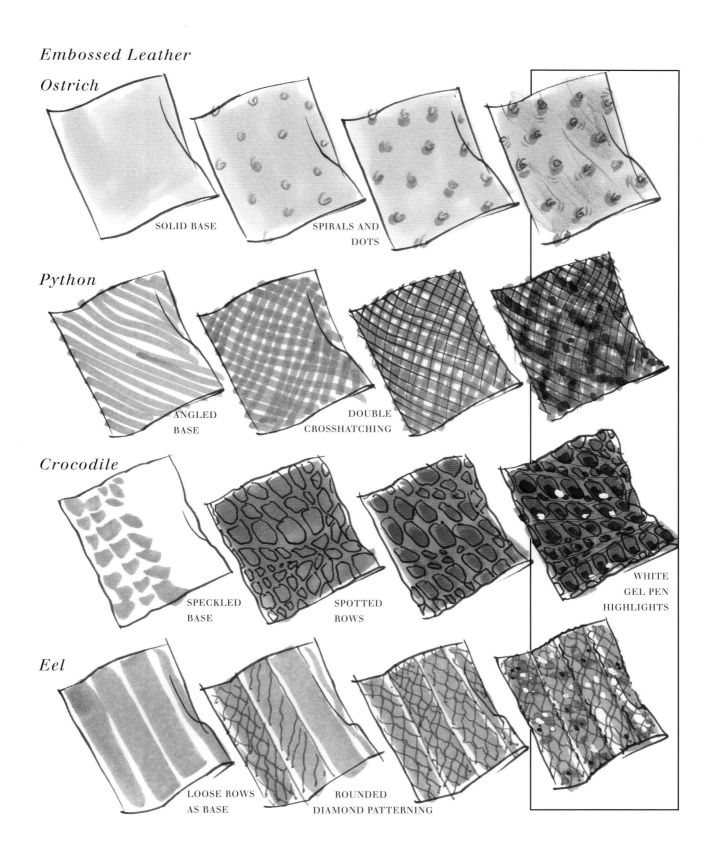

Embossed Leather

Ostrich

SOLID BASE

SPIRALS AND
DOTS

Python

ANGLED
BASE

DOUBLE
CROSSHATCHING

Crocodile

SPECKLED
BASE

SPOTTED
ROWS

WHITE
GEL PEN
HIGHLIGHTS

Eel

LOOSE ROWS
AS BASE

ROUNDED
DIAMOND PATTERNING

Home Fashions

Sometimes, when a sketch is small, a texture or print may have to be oversized or emphasized to convey the story of the material.

Accessories

With a lot of texture and detail fighting for attention in a small sketch, make sure your outline is dark and bold.

Jewelry

Often with fine metals or polished surfaces you'll have to leave room for shine (highlights) along with the texture and patterning for skin prints.

Fashion

Glossy materials can use a "wet" look—lots of light breaking into color. Work within the design detail and posing to capture the look.

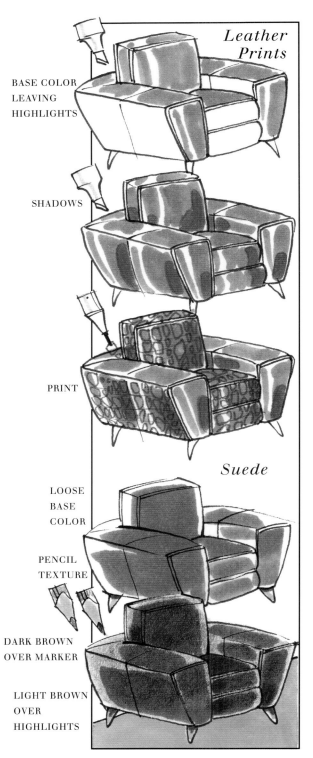

Leather Prints

BASE COLOR LEAVING HIGHLIGHTS

SHADOWS

PRINT

Suede

LOOSE BASE COLOR

PENCIL TEXTURE

DARK BROWN OVER MARKER

LIGHT BROWN OVER HIGHLIGHTS

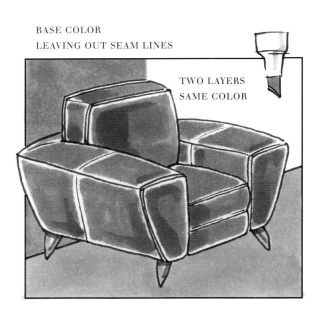

BASE COLOR LEAVING OUT SEAM LINES

TWO LAYERS SAME COLOR

Mock Crocodile

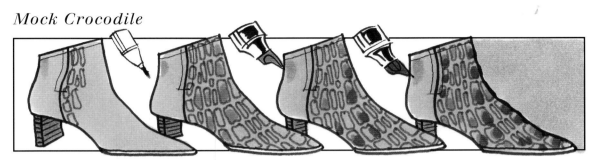

FOUR STEPS: BASE, PATTERN ROWS, TWO ACCENT COLORS

Faux Ostrich/Embossed Pigskin

FIVE STEPS: BASE, CONTRAST TRIM, SEMIDOTS, PENCIL GRAINLINES, GEL PEN ACCENTS

Lizard Print

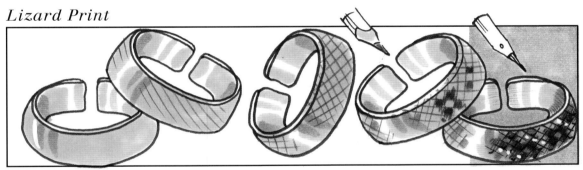

SIX STEPS: BASE, SHADOWS, GRID PATTERN, FOUR SKIN COLORS, GEL PEN ACCENTS

Glossy Leather/Pleather/Vinyl

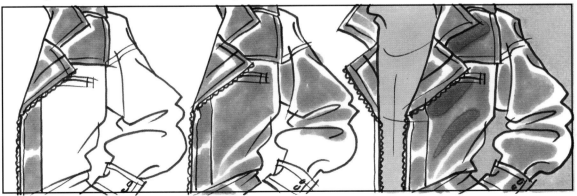

TWO STEPS: BASE, SHADOWS

Quilting

Quilting is more of a surface treatment than a texture. The stitching provides a type of pattern. The stuffing between the stitching provides the puffy look. Together the stitching and stuffing can appear subtle or pronounced, depending on the kind of quilting you're rendering. There are options in rendering here, from two to four steps. The one you use should be based on how much time you have to complete a sketch.

PARMA VIOLET

VIOLET

GRAY 70%

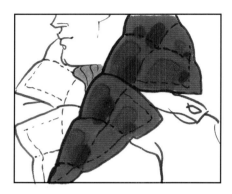

DEEP COLOR, NO HIGHLIGHTS

GLOSSY COLOR, GETS HIGHLIGHTS

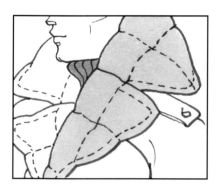

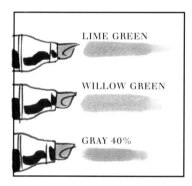

LIME GREEN

WILLOW GREEN

GRAY 40%

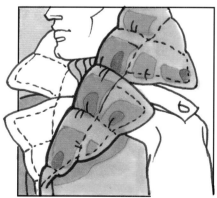

MATTE COLOR

LIGHT TAN, TWO LAYERS
GRAY 70% SHADING

THREE-STEP PUFFY QUILTING

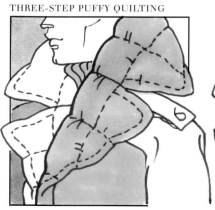

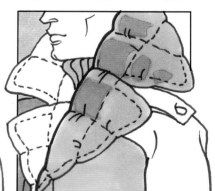

1. FLAT BACKGROUND

2. DEEPER COLOR FOR PUFF

3. SHADOW FOR DEPTH IN PUFF

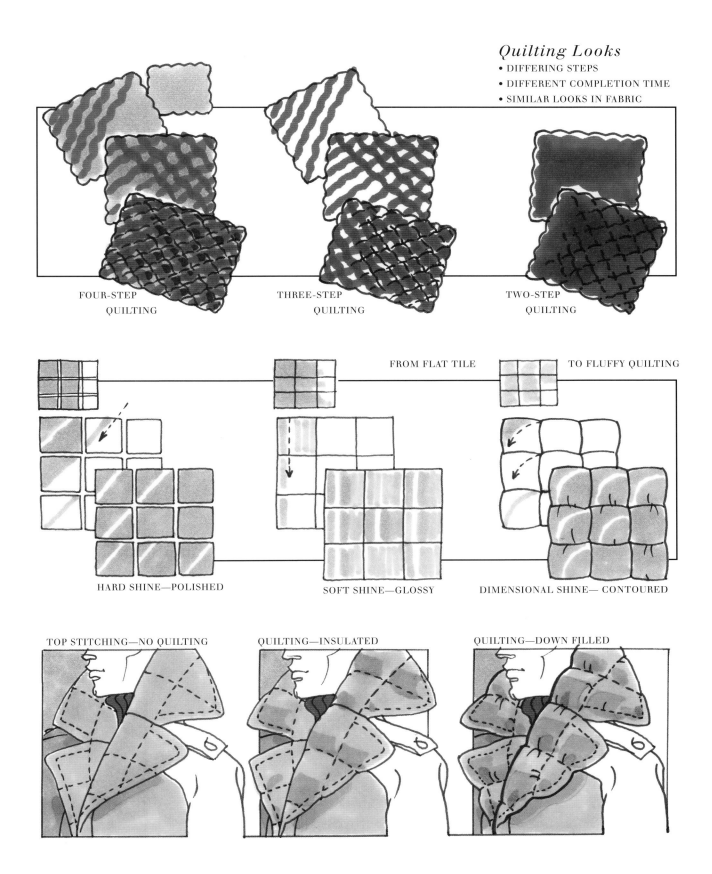

- DIFFERING STEPS
- DIFFERENT COMPLETION TIME
- SIMILAR LOOKS IN FABRIC

FOUR-STEP
QUILTING

THREE-STEP
QUILTING

TWO-STEP
QUILTING

FROM FLAT TILE

TO FLUFFY QUILTING

HARD SHINE—POLISHED

SOFT SHINE—GLOSSY

DIMENSIONAL SHINE— CONTOURED

TOP STITCHING—NO QUILTING

QUILTING—INSULATED

QUILTING—DOWN FILLED

Fall Fabrics

Mixing textures in fall fabrics, especially for children's wear, can run the gamut of smooth, nubby, rough, or fuzzy plus really shaggy for that kid's "cute" factor in clothes. Pen and pencil treatments on top of your marker become an integral part of your rendering process. Lush textured rendering can add to the sense of weight and bulk for fall fabrics that makes them look so different from spring fabrications.

BASE:	SHADING:	FUZZ:	TEXTURE 1.	TEXTURE 2.	TEXTURE 3.
VIOLET MIST	PARMA VIOLET	VIOLET	BLACK GRAPE	VIOLET BLUE	BLACK

MARKER BASE: TWO LAYERS

PENCIL FUZZ AND SHADING: ONE LAYER

PENCIL TEXTURE 1. TWO LAYERS

PENCIL TEXTURES 2 AND 3. FINISH THREE LAYERS

SATINY FINISH

CORDUROY ROWS

VINYL SHINE

ONE PENCIL: POINT

ONE PENCIL: SIDE

THREE PENCILS: POINTS AND SIDES

WOOL GABARDINE

WOOL FLANNEL

WOOL MELTON

You can substitute pen line dashes for shaggy hair lines in the wool melton.

Corduroy rows line up just the way stripes do. The rows get smudge lines like velvet does, yet corduroy has a look of its own. It can be crisp and tailored or soft and bulky depending on the width of the wale. Shape and construction factor in, too, by way of outline contours. Corduroy's interior texture depends on the nuance in your pencil technique over a marker base and shadow colors.

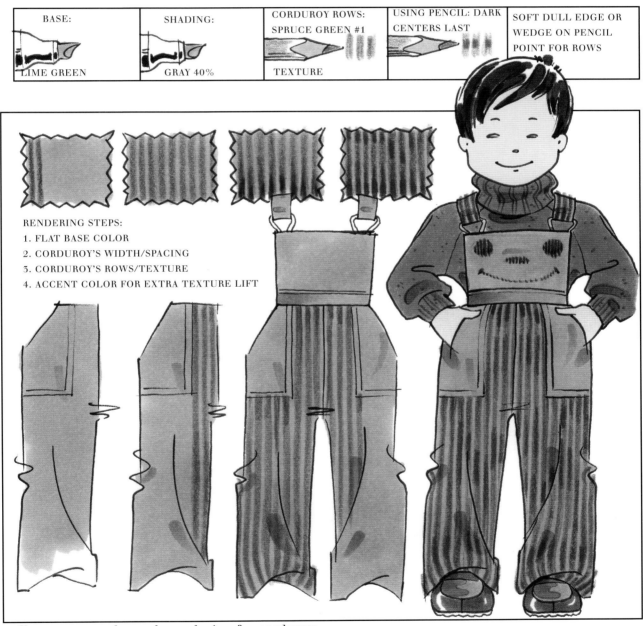

BASE:	SHADING:	CORDUROY ROWS: SPRUCE GREEN #1	USING PENCIL: DARK CENTERS LAST	SOFT DULL EDGE OR WEDGE ON PENCIL POINT FOR ROWS
LIME GREEN	GRAY 40%	TEXTURE		

RENDERING STEPS:
1. FLAT BASE COLOR
2. CORDUROY'S WIDTH/SPACING
3. CORDUROY'S ROWS/TEXTURE
4. ACCENT COLOR FOR EXTRA TEXTURE LIFT

You can use only marker coloring for corduroy
(no pencil). It just won't look as fuzzy.

Knits

Knits incorporate the looks of yarn types and patterns or knit motifs but not the actual stitches. Lightly pencil in rows to suggest a knit's overall ribbing. Get the knits to look stretchy or soft by adding a bit of cling to them using outline contour and placement of shadows. Use either a colored pencil or your outline pen line to create more specific knit stitches like cables or drop needle patterns.

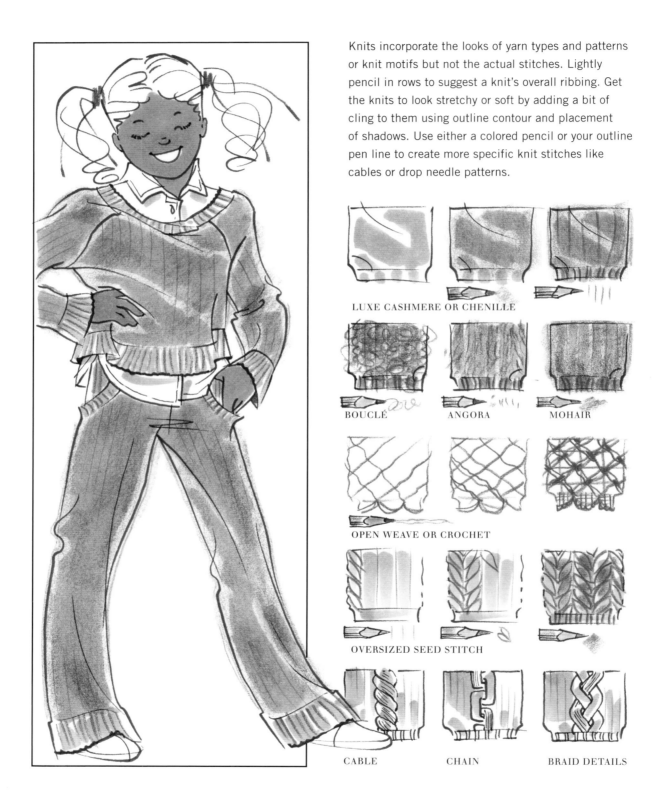

LUXE CASHMERE OR CHENILLE

BOUCLÉ   ANGORA   MOHAIR

OPEN WEAVE OR CROCHET

OVERSIZED SEED STITCH

CABLE   CHAIN   BRAID DETAILS

Heavyweight fall knits are meant to look bulky and warm. Despite the yarn thickness, you still want to build in some crush lines to keep the knit looking soft. To get a lift or to add dimension to some knit patterns, use a gray shadow on the repeat motifs.

Flat Color Knits

1. PEN LINE RIB AND KNIT PATTERN
2. MARKER BASE COLOR
3. SHADING TO EMPHASIZE KNIT PATTERN

Focus on Knit Rows

1. PEN OR PENCIL PATTERN
2. FOR COLOR BLOCKING, DO ONE COLOR AT A TIME IN ROWS WITH A FINE-POINT TIP
3. SKIP THE SHADING EXCEPT TO EMPHASIZE ANY THREE-DIMENSIONAL MOTIFS LIKE A POPCORN STITCH

Assignment

The many choices you have in illustrating different fabrics and the variety of textures and colors you can use may cause you stress. It can also make illustrating fun. Rendering shearling should be easy, like scribbling. Easy should be fun, and that's a good place to start to build your confidence in your skills.

- Start with your outline. Try it in black pen and brown pen and pencil. Get it as curly and loopy as you can.

- Work out your coloring technique to match the texture in your outline. Try different values to boost the look of the squiggly interior.
- Finish off with some pencil to add a bit of fuzziness to the color or to work in more curliness.
- Testing different methods always gives you more to analyze about what you do and don't like. This helps you develop your own style of drawing and rendering.

FABRIC REFERENCE

APPENDIX

1. CORDUROY

CHAPTERS 1, 4, 6, AND 7

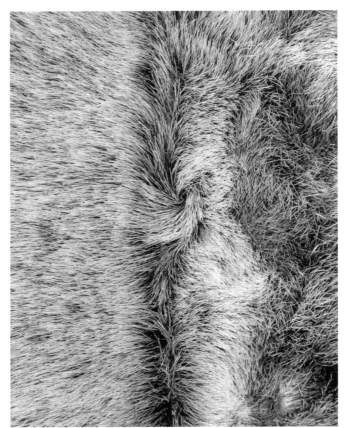

2. FAKE FUR

CHAPTER 7

3. STAMPED, EMBOSSED LEATHER AND SUEDES

CHAPTERS 1, 2, 6, AND 7

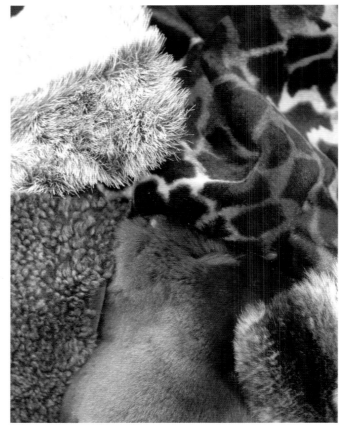

4. PLUSH ANIMAL PRINTS

CHAPTER 7

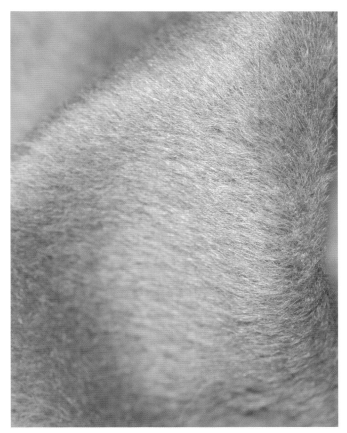

5. WOOL MELTON
   CHAPTERS 4 AND 7

6. ANIMAL PRINTS
   CHAPTER 7

7. ANIMAL AND SNAKE SKIN PRINTS
   CHAPTER 7

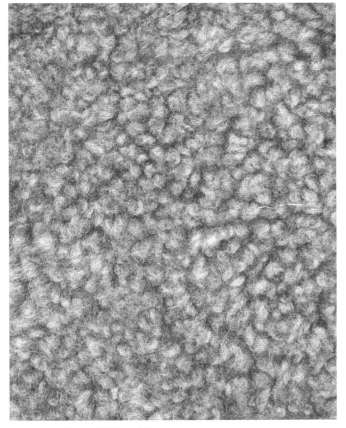

8. FAUX CURLY LAMB
   CHAPTER 7

9. GOLD LAMÉ AND METALLIC LACE
   CHAPTERS 1, 4, AND 6

10. BOUCLÉ
    CHAPTER 7

11. PLAID
    CHAPTERS 5 AND 6

12. HERRINGBONE
    CHAPTERS 1 AND 6

13. PAISLEY
CHAPTER 5

14. JACQUARD PRINTS
CHAPTERS 4, 5, AND 6

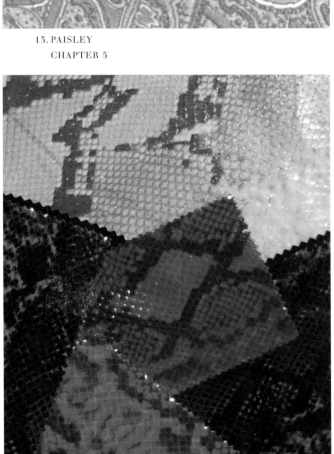

15. SNAKE SKIN PRINTS
CHAPTER 7

16. CHIFFON: CHAPTERS 4 AND 6
VELVET: CHAPTERS 1, 4, 5, AND 6
JACQUARD PRINT: CHAPTERS 4, 5, AND 6

17. DENIM AND CHAMBRAY
CHAPTER 6

18. ORGANZA
CHAPTERS 5 AND 6

19. TWEED (HERRINGBONE)
CHAPTERS 4 AND 6

20. STRIPE, CHECK, AND GINGHAM
CHAPTERS 1 AND 5

21. MOIRÉ TAFFETA
CHAPTERS 4 AND 6

22 PAINTED CHIFFON
CHAPTERS 4 AND 6

23. DAMASK
CHAPTERS 4 AND 6

24. CRUSHED VELVET
CHAPTER 4

25. GEOMETRIC PRINT
CHAPTER 5

26. CAMOUFLAGE
CHAPTER 5

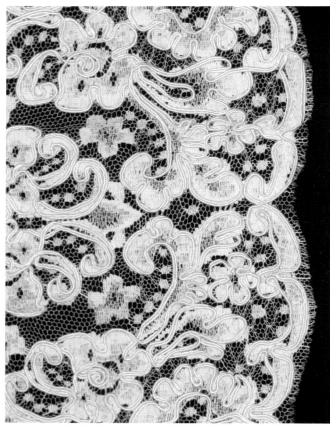

27. LACE
CHAPTERS 4 AND 6

28. HOUNDSTOOTH AND GLEN PLAID
CHAPTER 1

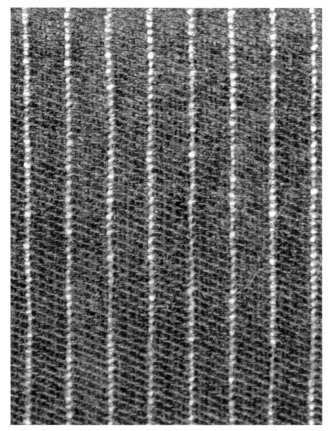

29. CHENILLE (PINSTRIPE)
CHAPTER 1

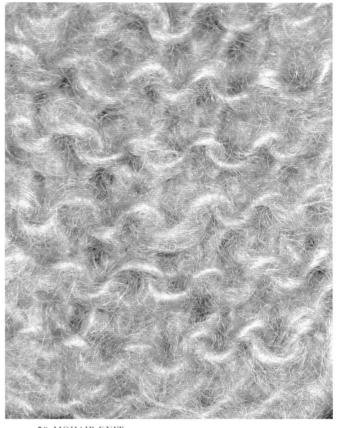

30. MOHAIR KNIT
CHAPTER 7

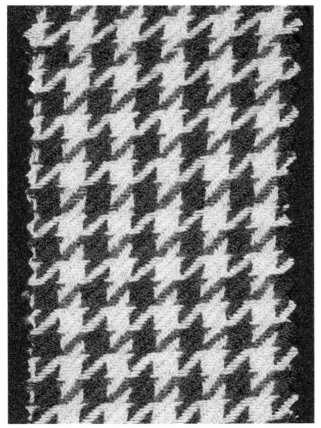

31. (OVERSIZED) HOUNDSTOOTH
CHAPTER 1

32. BASIC KNITS AND RIBBING
CHAPTERS 1, 5, 6, AND 7